Joel H. Silbey
Cornell University

THE
TRANSFORMATION
OF
AMERICAN
POLITICS,
1840-1860

Prentice-Hall, Inc., Englewood Cliffs, New Jersey

AMERICAN HISTORICAL SOURCES SERIES:
Research and Interpretation

LORMAN RATNER, Editor

PRENTICE-HALL INTERNATIONAL, INC., *London*
PRENTICE-HALL OF AUSTRALIA, PTY. LTD., *Sydney*
PRENTICE-HALL OF CANADA, LTD., *Toronto*
PRENTICE-HALL OF INDIA PRIVATE LTD., *New Delhi*
PRENTICE-HALL OF JAPAN, INC., *Tokyo*

To Rosemary

Current printing (last digit):
10 9 8 7 6 5 4 3 2 1

© 1967 by PRENTICE-HALL, INC.
Englewood Cliffs, New Jersey

Library of Congress Catalog Card No.: 67-28793

Printed in the United States of America

EDITOR'S FOREWORD

The Transformation of American Politics, 1840-1860 is a volume in the American Historical Sources Series, a series devoted to the exploration of aspects of American history and to the process of interpreting historical evidence. The introduction to each volume will be followed by some of the original documents used to prepare the essay. In this way readers are invited to share in the experience of turning raw evidence into history. The essay has been written especially for this series and represents a contribution to historical knowledge as well as a demonstration of how history is written.

Between the elections of 1840 and those of 1860 American political parties went through a series of profound shifts in leadership, principles, and programs. The changes in the makeup of the parties reflected changes in the economic, ethnic, and cultural faces of America. While certainly concerned about such issues as slavery and states rights, Americans were also disturbed by the sudden and massive influx of immigrants, the revolution in the nature and tempo of economic life, and the changes, real and imagined, in traditional American values and beliefs that either were occurring or that they believed would occur. Faced with new and basic issues, Americans had to determine where they stood and with whom. So important were these issues and so drastically did political groups realign that the parties of 1840 shifted markedly and were replaced by political organizations cemented by new leaders and based on new principles and programs.

Historians, in relating developments of the decades from 1840 to 1860 to the Civil War, have understressed this political transformation and the issues that caused it. Professor Silbey has examined these decades away from the shadow of the Civil War and made us aware that immigration and economic change which so occupied Americans' attention in the post-war decades were of major importance before the war. Some recent historians have warned of the danger of allowing the Civil War to act as an absolute divider of American History. Professor Silbey joins that group.

LORMAN RATNER

iii

CONTENTS

part five
THE REPUBLICAN COALITION
108

Politics and Society: The Process of Political Change

In the presidential election of 1840 the Whig and Democratic parties bitterly contested for control of the American government. Each party's campaign was shaped in large part by their different responses to the problems posed by the depression in which the country had been sunk since 1837; each advocated quite contrasting policies as solutions to the economic crisis. At the same time each party pushed other policies as well, many of which were rooted in the conflicts of Andrew Jackson's presidency. Both received from the electorate substantial popular support based on the attraction of their programs, their candidates, or the meaning each had to each voter. In the wake of a spirited campaign and a large popular turnout, the Whigs won control of Congress, and their candidate, William Henry Harrison, captured the presidency. Twenty years later, in 1860, the descendants and heirs of the contesting groups of 1840 fought another bitter presidential election. This time the Republican Party won its first national election and placed Abraham Lincoln in the Executive Mansion.

But there basic similarities ended, for there were fundamental differences between the two elections beyond the different victorious parties. In the two decades between elections, in response to the rapid growth of the United States and the changes caused by that growth, some new or formerly understressed problems demanded solution. Some of these issues were similar to those fought over in 1840, others, however, were not. The rhetoric of politics, the issues at the center of the stage, and the vital concerns of those involved in politics had all significantly changed. Groups which had been Democrats in 1840 were so no longer; former Whigs were now Democrats. Some people remained steadfast, but many others shifted their partisan support in response to the challenge of new conditions and issues. Partisan attachments are usually so tenaciously held by those who participate in politics that the great amount of shifting loyalties and abandoning of previous commitments during this period constituted a significant transformation of American politics. Furthermore, the impact of that transformation stretched beyond the period in which it occurred to affect political life right into the twentieth century, despite subsequent social and political changes. In some cases certain aspects of the transformation of 1840-1860 are still firmly imbedded in modern American politics.

American historians have maintained a persistent interest in the twenty years before the Civil War, focusing particularly on the conditions which produced that violent outbreak. Although historiographic interpretations of the causes of secession and war have undergone many shifts of emphasis and consequent revision in the last century, they have been united on one basic theme: the relationship of the major political conflicts of the country to the development of the conditions producing the Civil War. They have generally viewed the issues dividing the American people either as part of the developing sectional conflict or as relatively insignificant and temporary. Thus, such matters as immigration between 1840 and 1860, have often been treated as basically unrelated to the central concerns of the period, or have been fitted in as aspects of the larger sectional contest. The result of 100 years of historical concern about the coming of the war is therefore a picture of the American scene dominated by a basic sectional conflict and of the American people increasingly, almost exclusively, preoccupied with the conditions that led to the break of 1861.

Without going into the question of how historians have determined the central focus of the prewar era, we can still consider the problem posed by another matter already referred to, the change in American voting patterns, and ask several questions about it. First, how much was it related to the conditions leading toward war? How much was it a product of other and unrelated forces present? And, what do the first two answers tell us about the period under review on one hand, and the general nature of American political behavior on the other? We may frame the questions in this way because at the same time that the drama of secession unfolded, the humdrum of American politics continued with some profound rumblings that probably were not aspects of the conditions creating a war situation. In recent years systematic analysts of American politics have begun to examine with some care why people vote as they do in historic situations. These analysts have shown that the answer is often highly complex and often unrelated to the alleged great issues of the day, or not as affected by them as by other matters also present. Such findings suggest new bases for understanding the nature of American social processes and historical development as well as provide insights into why the Civil War erupted as it did. In the following pages, therefore, the intention is to introduce some of the factors present in the period which apparently had some major political effects as keys to a larger understanding of the total political process in the past history of the United States. In a work as brief as this, of course, we can only establish the basic structure of what occurred and can discuss and illustrate only guideposts of a much larger process.

I

Throughout our history the American people have responded in their political behavior to a wide range of influences which have shaped and determined their actions. From the fight over the ratification of the Constitution to the most recent presidential election, incidents of sectional and local loyalties, the desire to defend some particular institution held dear, a concern for economic well-being, fear of the presence or growing power of some unsympathetic group or individual, locality, or foreign nation have all played a role in determining particular group behavior. The United States has always been a most heterogeneous society where the many different and often conflicting individuals contend for those things each believes will "maximize . . . [his] satisfactions." * Each defines his satisfactions through the group and environment in which he is nurtured, and whose values, outlooks, and experiences he has absorbed. Their traditions, goals, fears, antagonisms, ideology, and politics become his reference points to the world outside and the bases of his social and political behavior.

The group, in turn, moves into politics in pursuit of its political

* Lee Benson, "Some Crude Generalizations about American Voting Behavior," in *The Concept of Jacksonian Democracy* (Princeton, N.J.: Princeton University Press, 1961).

goals as it acts to promote beneficial policies or to forestall measures deemed harmful to it. If one wants some specific economic aid, a particular tariff provision for example, political action is necessary to influence the government to take action. On the other side of the same issue, if one does not want that particular tariff provision to pass he must also engage in political activity to prevent it. Similarly, if an individual perceives some threat to his idea of correct social order, stemming from the presence or power of some other group, the Congregationalists of an established Church, or Irish Catholics, or Whigs, for example, political action may ameliorate that threat. In other words, individuals through their life associations acquire an idea of the world and seek to preserve and promote that idea, especially against attempts to limit or destroy it. Since such ideas emerge out of ethnic, religious, economic, sectional, or local associations, and since there are many of these in the United States, there are always disagreements as to what is the correct social order and consequently what policies the government should pursue.

To carry out one's desires, or to fulfill one's perceived role, or to orient oneself toward other groups in the society, some institutional framework, some coalition of allied interests is often necessary so that sufficient power may be exerted to sway government policy in particular directions. In most representative systems of government political parties have been that institutional framework. Various groups who can agree about certain policies or who jointly oppose other policies, coalesce to promote their interests. Such coalescence is not easily accomplished as the groups strive to agree on priorities and policies and conciliate potential disagreements. But once the shakedown period has passed, the parties develop a unified and stable outlook and a mass of loyal adherents. During the Jacksonian period two such national coalitions had formed and bitterly fought one another for control of the government apparatus in pursuit of the particular desires of their component groups. By the 1840's both parties were firmly entrenched in American life. Each was meeting in some decided fashion the political requirements of its constituent groups and thus maintaining their loyalty. But, as we have noted, by 1860 the situation had changed markedly: one of the objects of this loyalty, the Whig party had disappeared; the other, the Democratic party, had greatly changed in its composition and outlook. And a new party had gained control of the government.

The political change of the ante-bellum period was the outgrowth of changing conditions in American life and the failure of the traditional parties to cope with these changes adequately. Several groups, particularly in the Democratic party, grew increasingly restive about their party's position on matters such as economic growth, immigration, religious affairs, and the extension of slavery. Ultimately, as these issues became more salient, that is, more important to them, several of the groups shifted politically in order to restore the necessary conditions for maximizing their satisfactions. Concern over these issues was powerful enough to weaken the strongest of traditional partisan loyalties. The result was the emergence of the Republican party and a change in the nature of the Democratic party. Those historians who have thought the reasons for this political shift to be rooted in the growing sectional conflict over slavery have also noted the presence of political groups who were indifferent to slavery or more interested in other matters, particularly cultural and economic issues. The Republican leaders shrewdly played upon these other matters, in addition to discussing slavery, and sought the best combination of the various issues in order to build their party. The Republican victory of 1860 resulted from no single-minded devotion to any one issue, but from an appeal based on the right combination of ethnocultural, economic, and moral proposals designed to meet the changed needs and desires of a combination of social groups.

Issues involving religious differences, temperance, and slavery, which grew more salient to many people between 1840 and 1860, had not been entirely absent from earlier elections. Occasionally even, in special circumstances, they had been important factors in influencing some voting decisions. The difference between the periods before 1840 and the subsequent decades was the shift in emphasis away from earlier matters and the high priority assigned to these new matters. Such shifting is the very stuff of political change. In 1840 the hangover from the Jacksonian period and its issues played a most significant role, heightened by a depression and its consequent economic distress. By 1860, although there had just been another depression, there were also other elements, for example the alien-Catholic upsurge, which many people viewed as the central problem of the day. Because of this shift in perspective, the Republican party emerged to a position of national power. In the remainder of this essay we will focus on the specific components of this political shift, first by establishing the pattern of American politics in the early 1840's and then by discussing how and why the political changes referred to actually took place.

II

"Two great rival hosts now divide the American people," Horace Greeley wrote in 1843, introducing his editorial, "The Grounds of Difference Between the Contending Parties," (included below as Source 1), "and by their struggles for ascendency agitate and . . . convulse the nation." The convulsions centered primarily on economic matters: the parties disagreed over such things as tariff policy, banks, internal improvements, and public land disposal. The emphasis is not surprising in light of the battles of the 1830's over economic policy, which had contributed significantly to the formation of the Whig party and the stabilizing of the Democratic coalition, or of the effects of the depression which had plagued American life since 1837. Groups in the electorate had disagreed over the needed solutions to everything from tariffs to how to end the depression and promote economic growth. Each national coalition, in response, had absorbed and built upon these disagreements, each holding one set of ideas devoutly and promoting them actively. To the Democrats, the central tenets of their faith included low tariffs, an independent treasury, low land prices, limited government operations to keep expenditures down, and little if any federal sponsorship of internal improvements construction. On the other hand, the Whigs made it clear that proper policy involved a protective tariff, a centralized national bank, federal aid for internal improvements, and other necessary expansion of government power to meet the needs of the American people.

Although these items were the meat of the platforms of the two parties in the early 1840's occasionally other issues were also discussed. Some of these, territorial expansion, for one, divided the parties in the same way as economic issues had. The Democrats generally favored, the Whigs usually opposed, a policy of aggressive territorial expansion, and these attitudes quickly became incorporated into party platforms. Other issues, for example items involving slavery and Negro rights, provoked sectional, not party divisions. These, however, were quite unusual in this period and not a major part of the political scene. All of these issues pointed to another characteristic of American politics in the early 1840's: the system was dominated by a strong nationality. Both parties were national in scope, well supported in every state and section, each winning a share of the local, state, and national political offices, and each receiving a substantial popular vote throughout the country. Of course there were some political leaders who viewed sectional, not national questions, as the important matters of the day. Their presence was later to be highly important in American politics but in the early 1840's their outlook only produced frustration, which revealed their political impotence. The party spokesmen made it quite clear that if a national issue contained a sectional component, the former would prevail, and they would be swayed by their partisan not their sectional commitment. "Better the evils of slavery for a season," the editor of a Northern newspaper wrote when warned about the extension of slavery if the United States annexed Texas, "than British domination forever." The simple fact was that the basic components of party differences, such issues as the bank or tariff, knew no section, and so long as they remained the central issues of the day, sectional inclinations received little hearing.

The national party divisions over government policy were not confined to the rhetorical realm. Congress acted on most of these issues during the 1830's and 1840's and exhibited a high degree of party loyalty over them. In their speeches, but most importantly, in their voting, the congressmen divided along party lines in support of the various proposals. Of course there were defections from the party coalitions at times, but these were by individuals or small groups rarely representing more than a small minority of the whole party bloc in Congress. The persistent party adherence of the majority underlined the role parties played in American politics and the high degree of loyalty to them as the main instruments for achieving policy goals, helping individuals to fulfill desired roles, and aligning their components in relation to other groups in the electorate. Representative Howell Cobb's strong affirmation of his Democracy in his 1848 speech (Source 2) dramatized the intensity of that partisan commitment, with its rejection of the view that any other organization could possibly do for Cobb what his party had and would do. Simply stated, party disaffection was quite foreign to a man like Cobb, nurtured, as he had been, in the prevailing highly partisan political system. William Pitt Fessenden, a Whig stalwart displayed the same intensity, commenting that he "would vote for a dog, if he was the candidate of my party."

This, then, was the American political situation at the beginning of the 1840's: a national political structure overlaying a series of sharp policy differences; a highly developed institutional framework, to which those involved in politics maintained a tenacious loyalty, and one in which, to the contemporary observer, there was a degree of permanence which precluded any hope of far-reaching changes in it. Horace Greeley, constantly hamstrung in his efforts to wean Democratic voters away from their leaders, unhappily noted that the latter "may have a roast baby for breakfast every morning, with missionary steaks for dinner, and yet rule the country forever." But they did not rule the country forever, or for very long. The immigrant, the Negro, and the economic entrepreneur unwittingly combined to bring about the downfall of the Democrats. All of the factors in the transformation operated simultaneously with each other, but the issue of the alien immigrant opened up one of the oldest of social sores in this country, never entirely absent, even during the period of national political institutions.

III

"Now," wrote the editor of the *Detroit Free Press* in 1856, "there are three factions in this state combined against the Democratic party . . . : the Maine liquor law faction; the religious test faction, otherwise called know-nothings; and the anti-slavery faction." The editor's stress on ethnocultural tensions emphasized their suddenly increased relevance in American politics in the middle 1850's. We have noted that an underlying influence on political behavior is the group identification of individual voters and their positive or negative reactions toward other social groups. In this country, the most pervasive group identification and rejection pattern involves ethnic and religious associations. There has been an enduring element of hostility, hatred, and open conflict between the different national and religious groups in the American melting pot. Inexorably, from the beginning of the Republic onward these tensions have spilled over into politics, often to play a most significant role in shaping mass voting behavior. Before the 1850's, however, despite clear manifestations of cultural group hostilities in politics, they were never sufficiently salient to influence politics on a national scale. Lee Benson's study of New York voting behavior in 1844 indicates political cohesiveness by some cultural groups, but splintering between Whigs and Democrats by others, indicating that factors other than cultural identification were more influential. "The conditions," Benson said, "which would lead the native Protestant electorate to respond politically to nativist, anti-Catholic issues had not yet developed during the 1840's." Ten years later this was no longer the case. Then a nativist movement powerful enough to significantly weaken many traditional political loyalties had developed as the prelude to the beginning of a political transformation.

In the late 1840's, in reaction to suddenly worsened economic and political conditions in Europe, floods of immigrants, particularly from Ireland and Germany, began to move into the United States. Most of the poverty-stricken Irish settled in the Eastern port cities. The Germans mainly moved west into the Upper Mississippi Valley. The statistics of the migration indicate its size: between 1848 and 1860 almost three and a half million migrants entered the United States. In 1853 alone, over 368,000 came, more than 300,000 Irish and Germans among them. In Boston the number of naturalized voters increased between 1850 and 1855 by about 300 per cent, the native-born voters increased only 14 per cent; the naturalized, mostly Irish, made up one-third of the city's electorate in 1855. The immigrant's numbers, presence, and potential power were enough to arouse latent ethnic and religious antagonisms and provoke a most serious reaction. As early as 1849, the editor of *The American Protestant Magazine* warned that the "emigrants will soon overcome us." As increasing numbers of native-born Americans agreed, they began to search for some way to control, reverse, or repel, the sudden social problem they perceived.

It was not just the immigrant himself as an individual or as part of a particular national group that frightened many Americans. Rather they worried over what the growing alien presence portended for traditional American values and institutions. As John Sanderson wrote in his book, *Republican Landmarks* (Source 3), these immigrants knew little of American republican practices, and yet they soon participated in them through the ballot, usually to further their own narrow ethnic concerns. The national Democratic party, seeking votes wherever it could, pandered to the immigrant, used his voting power, often illegally, and then supported the immigrant's particular interests regardless of what was best for the country. The immigrants, themselves, in their irrational state, brought to American political life much violence and licentiousness in the name of some vaguely defined "liberty." There were riots at polling places, immigrant bloc voting, illegalities, payoffs, and corruption in abundance. There was a definite need for some organized political action by native Americans in defense of traditional American values before the alien-Democratic alliance destroyed American republicanism and liberty.

The political threat posed by the immigrant was by no means the only danger. His national background, his practices, and his general conduct when he reached our shores, the Reverend Samuel Busey demonstrated (Source 4), severely affected and threatened the social fabric of the whole nation. In the wake of the vast increase of aliens, there had been increases in crime, pauperism, "disease, disorder, and immorality." A careful reading of the published reports of urban social conditions quickly demonstrated the source of the increase. A larger proportion of immigrants than native-born Americans were paupers, lunatics, and criminals, and generated the higher incidences of the conditions of social decay. Nor was that all. The large numbers of immigrants seeking welfare aid from local and religious authorities had drained available funds sharply and threatened the collapse of the whole system. Many native poor would therefore be deprived of their only source of support. The same was true in regard to prisons. The rise in immigrant crime had increased the need for prison facilities with another major drain on state and local funds. Given such facts, Busey argued, the immigrant tide, unless controlled, ultimately would so weaken the social system as to destroy the country.

There was a third problem connected with the coming of the immigrant which awakened the most fears of all. Rooted in the Protestant dissent spawned by the Reformation, and heir to the English fears of the Roman Catholic Church, the American people had traditionally manifested a deeply rooted anti-Catholicism. From Puritan Massachusetts Bay to mid-nineteenth-century Boston, there were persistent popular fears of conspiracies led by Catholics against Protestant America. The depravities of the Catholic clergy were also much stressed. Maria Monk's story of her escape from a Montreal convent in a pregnant condition due to the activities of bestial priests titillated many Americans in the early 1830's. Pandering to some of the most devotedly held components of anti-Catholic ideology, such stories occasionally produced violence against Catholic churches and convents, and invasions of the latter in search of forcibly held Protestant girls.

The relevance of all of this lies in the sharp upsurge of anti-Catholic feeling caused by the immigrant influx of the 1850's. The Irish, and many of the Germans as well, were of the hated religion, and the Catholic Church became more visible than ever before as it built up its organization here to serve its increased number of communicants. To many Americans, this growth of the Church's structure was the prelude to subversion and national destruction. William Brownlow, a Methodist minister in Tennessee, was only one of many who called attention to the danger. In *Americanism Contrasted with Foreignism, Romanism, and Bogus Democracy* (Source 5) he bitterly castigated Catholicism for its immorality, false doctrine, and its drive to conquer the world, which had now reached our shores. He pointed to the most dangerous fact, that the Church's establishment in the United States was now larger than in the British Isles, a sufficient indication of the spreading danger.

As the Catholic threat spread with the increased hordes of immigrants, nativist leaders sought effective remedial action. Some Protestant ministers advocated extensive missionary activity among the aliens to turn them from their Catholicism. "If we would save ourselves, we must save the Emigrant," was a persistent theme. Unfortunately the Catholic aliens proved unreceptive to Protestant salvation and frustrated the hopes of the religious reformers. Increasingly and inevitably, therefore, as argument and persuasion failed, political action was employed to ameliorate the threat. Such action had to begin with the overthrow of the Democratic party with its corrupt alliance with "priest controlled machines," and its control of the national government.

The association of the Democratic party with subversive foreign groups was not new among nativists. The Alien and Sedition acts of the late 1790's were enacted partly in response to the increased power of the Jeffersonian Republicans and their alien supporters. Later, in the middle 1830's in New York City, local Whig organizations frankly adopted parts of the programs pushed by local nativist associations. In 1840, a Whig-dominated New York Legislature passed an alien registry law, severely limiting the political rights of naturalized citizens. Other manifestations of common Whig/nativist attitudes and associations were frequently displayed. In fact, in the wake of their defeat in the presidential election of 1844, one Whig leader had suggested that they change the party's name to the American party, shift the focus of their appeal to outright nativism, and thus attract to them the native-born Democrats who had not yet realized the dangers threatened by alien power.

None of these political movements were very successful in hurting the Democrats until the middle 1850's when the growing concern over the rising number of immigrants exploded into a political force strong enough to threaten the hegemony of the Democratic party in the Northern states. This new nativist movement appeared first on the state level centering around what was, for a long time, the particular symbol of cultural conflict: liquor consumption and temperance reform. Although most nativist groups themselves rarely abstained from the use of alcoholic spirits of varying strength, they now began to perceive a significant social danger in the increased alcohol consumption in this country. As the Reverend Rufus Clark wrote in his defense of a Massachusetts temperance law (Source 6), most of the social evils rising from the violence, insanity, pauperism, and vice in the United States could be directly traced to the baneful effects of alcoholic consumption. Drunkenness produced debasement, and since the manufacture and sale of spirits produced drunkenness, the liquor trade had to be halted in order to save society itself.

What gave Clark's appeal particular relevance at this moment was the association of the immigrant with the increased traffic in alcoholic spirits. The Germans, for example, introduced lager beer into the United States on a widespread basis, which removed the previously limiting factor of price from alcohol consumption and made it everywhere readily available. The Irish were also stereotyped as intemperately excessive consumers. The immigrants, moreover, in contrast to the Puritan conception of the Sabbath as a day of quiet contemplation, looked upon Sunday as their day of relaxation, Sabbath or not. The spread of "grog shops" and beer gardens "like the frogs of Egypt" with their Sunday openings was quickly and unfavorably noted in the nativist press. As the editors of the *American Protestant Magazine* wrote in 1849 (Source 7), nine-tenths of the bars of New York City were owned by foreigners and were a "great and growing evil," as they sped the descent of the alien into that social degradation which ultimately caused violent difficulties for the rest of the population.

Their concern about the effects of alien drinking habits led many nativist political groups to seek to enact temperance laws to end "the curse of legalized rum-selling," as the first step in the social reforms of the country. The growing intensity of the issue can be seen in the widespread success of the movement. The Maine legislature led the way and most other Northern state legislatures followed and passed the necessary limiting laws. In most states it was the Whigs who took up the issue and fought for temperance, the Democrats who opposed such laws as a deprivation of individual liberties. Alien spokesmen joined the Democratic leadership in attacking "the temperance swindle" and the "Puritan bigotry" of the "Sunday and Cold Water fanatics" who led the restrictive movement. The Whigs, however, found in the movement a prime means of breaking the Democratic hold on the machinery of government. The political coalitions formed behind temperance quickly transcended party lines as a significant number of Democrats of native Protestant stock pulled away from their traditional moorings to support the nativists in the middle 1850's. The Maine Law, one Democratic leader remarked, had been "a curse to the Democratic party and produced a schism which puzzles the wisest heads to get rid of."

The conditions producing the political schism did not end with the passage of the temperance laws. Aliens were still entering the country in large numbers, and the Democrats in power in Washington still ignored that social threat. National political action based on the nativist coalition that had succeeded on the temperance issue clearly was the next step. Since the Democrats were unwilling, and the Whigs too weak, to carry out a program of immigrant restriction, the nativist leaders set out on an independent path by forming the American or Know-Nothing party. That grouping won some startling victories in the middle 1850's and ran a presidential candidate in 1856 on a platform which called attention to America's danger and outlined the steps necessary to prevent an alien-Catholic takeover in the face of Democratic indifference and Whig hesitancy (Source 8).

The Know-Nothing movement had a brief life as an independent political force, splitting apart on the rock of sectional issues. The party suffered the same fate as other single-idea political movements in our history. They did not offer enough within a complex society to attract a permanent following. Their best ideas were therefore appropriated by others as part of a larger complex of issues. People might hate and fear the immigrant yet be concerned about tariff rates and slavery too. The Know-Nothings, conscious of the diverse political groupings within their ranks, hesitated to take strong stands on other matters, fearing division. Therefore, many Northern Know-Nothings walked out of the party as the newly formed Republican party not only adopted a nativist tinge but also talked about other things of moment. By that time, however, the Know-Nothings had contributed a great deal to the developing political transformation. They had shaken loose from their mooring many traditional political groups, not only Whigs but Democrats as well. Most of these had no place to go now, except to the Republicans. The Republican leaders did not hesitate to woo the nativist-oriented groups either. Goodlove Orth, an Indiana Republican, wrote to a colleague that "we must not lose sight of the fact that while there is a strong anti-slavery feeling in the state, there is also a strong American feeling—and both must be preserved and united if possible, else both go by the board." Orth recognized, as did others, that most groups who opposed the alien, were also attracted to the anti-slavery movement, and had earlier supported the Whig party on other grounds. The anti-Democratic tone of nativism paralleled similar sentiment among anti-slavery reformers and former Whigs. Thus there was a strong possibility for common action.

In some places nativist-Republican associations were under way as early as 1854. Neal Dow, the leader of Maine's temperance forces, recalled how his group, the Know-Nothings, the Free-Soilers, and the anti-slavery extension Democrats, all met in the same cities at the same time in the spring and summer of 1854 (Source 9). They exchanged support for each other's ideas and candidates and moved a long step toward unity, which, because of their common interests, background, and objectives, they were able to accomplish during one gubernatorial campaign. In other states similar joint meetings also occurred. As a result of the association efforts, many of the leading Know-Nothings, Henry Wilson and Nathaniel Banks, for example, soon became Republican leaders. More importantly, the nascent Republican organization officially adopted nativist principles. In Indiana, for example, the Republican platform contained a strong Maine Law statement and a more cautious, but still strong nativist voting plank (Source 10). Other state Republican platforms contained similar planks. And, when the party achieved power it often carried out aspects of the nativist program. In Massachusetts, in 1859, the Republican Legislature passed a law preventing naturalized citizens from exercising their voting or office-holding rights for two years after their naturalization. This law was to have some nation-wide negative repercussions for the Republicans the following year, but stands unrivalled as a climactic example of the association of nativist sentiment with the Republican party.

On the other side of the political spectrum, and despite defections from their party by native Protestant groups, Democratic leaders maintained their opposition to immigration restriction. In Congress, through editorials and in public speeches, Democratic spokesmen attacked the Know-Nothings and blasted the Republicans for associating with and adopting them (Source 11). To the immigrant who might be attracted to Republicanism on other grounds, an editor warned that the party was nothing but a "Maine-Law, Native-American, Anti-Catholic . . ." grouping led by former Know-Nothings. In various resolutions of party meetings, the Democrats clearly established the contrast between themselves as the party of liberalism and traditional American friendship for the immigrant and the Republicans' hostility and restrictiveness (Source 12). Such counterblasts also paved the way for the many political fights of the late 1850's between the Republicans and Democrats on the issue which often became the determinative factor in many races.

The controversy over the immigrant, with its political consequences, was the first of the several strands that knotted together in the twenty years before 1860 to transform American politics. The reaction of many Americans against aliens, particularly Catholics, in the 1850's, generated a major movement involving both positive and negative reference group behavior in defense of particular life styles against threatened assaults from uncongenial groups. Lee Benson has argued that these "nativist, anti-Catholic movements were largely responsible for the political revolution that began in 1854." Certainly one can perceive how the Republican party built up much long-lasting support among the nativist/anti-alien groups it attracted as the successor to the temperance and Know-Nothing movements. Still there were those in the political spectrum affected less, apparently, by these cultural problems alone, than by other things. A look at some of these other matters will round out the picture of the change in the American political system before 1860.

IV

By 1840 slavery had existed for over two centuries on the American continent. During that period there had been recurring attacks on it as an anomaly within a free society, and an increasingly organized attempt to abolish it. At the beginning of the 1840's, slavery was confined to the southern states, while, in the North, an organized abolitionist movement railed against it and the South in newspapers, sermons, speeches, and fervently phrased pamphlets. Southerners were obviously quite hostile to the abolitionists and their appeal, but they had little to fear then. Not many people in the North responded favorably to the abolitionists nor demonstrated any great interest in the plight of the enslaved African. James Birney, the presidential candidate of the abolitionist-sponsored Liberty Party, received few votes in either 1840 or 1844. Most Northerners were too concerned about other matters, too hostile to the Negro, and too loyal to their national parties, with their southern wings, to endorse such a sectional movement. The tendency was, therefore, to play down and ignore slavery and to look upon the abolitionists as trouble makers and not as harbingers of greater freedom. The anti-slavery movement itself split in its frustration, lack of success, and inability to reconcile the conflicting forces within it.

Suddenly, in the middle 1840's, there was a decided change in the fortune of the anti-slavery movement. The abolitionists themselves were not adopted, but some of their ideas were. One of the central tenets of their faith was a belief in a slaveholder's conspiracy to control the American government and to use it for the promotion of slavery extension. In the aftermath of America's move westward in the middle 1840's, a series of legislative and executive defeats for non-slaveholding interests, and the belief that southern leaders had played a prominent role in those reverses, pumped life into and gave a measure of reality to the accusation. We had acquired all of Texas with its large number of slaves and its potentiality for future slave expansion there. We were about to go to war with Mexico, a conflict produced by our annexation of Texas. At the same time, the Tennessean President Polk compromised our Oregon boundary dispute with England, rather than run the risk of war with that power. We lost all of Oregon north of the 49th parallel despite the belief of many Westerners in our just claim to the area. Congress supported the southern-born President's compromising action as several Westerners walked out of the House chamber chanting "Fifty-four forty forever." Congress also sustained Polk in his veto of the western-sponsored internal improvements bill of 1846 (see Part Five), another apparent victory for southern interests and defeat for non-southern needs. Such a series of events seemingly convinced some Northerners of the correctness of the earlier abolitionist charge, and they moved to the attack.

Slaveholders, in common with other Americans, looked to the new lands acquired in California and New Mexico as a result of the war with Mexico, as major sources of future growth and wealth. Some northern congressmen, however, led by Representative David Wilmot of Pennsylvania, now declared their opposition to the opening of these and any subsequently acquired lands to slavery. Many of these Northerners were probably genuinely anti-slavery; others were moved by their conviction that the South had misused its power and wanted to punish that section. Whatever their motives, and despite the fact that there is little evidence that a conscious slaveholders conspiracy did actually exist, Wilmot introduced his anti-slavery extension Proviso into Congress in August, 1846. In a speech shortly after its appearance, Wilmot detailed the reasons for the Proviso in a sharply-worded attack on southern power in the Union (Source 13). Slaveholders, he said, had continually acted for their own parochial interests and against the welfare of the rest of the country. Something such as the Proviso was necessary therefore, to prevent them from building up their political power any further and using it to run rampant over the interests of everyone else. In this and subsequent statements, neither Wilmot nor his supporters threatened, as had the abolitionists, slavery's right to exist where it already did, nor did they challenge the property rights of slaveholders, nor threaten them with social upheaval, all of which frightened as many Northerners as Southerners and probably limited the appeal of the abolitionists in the nonslaveholding states. The Provisoists took, instead, quite pragmatic ground, emphasizing their primary interest in the welfare of northern farmers, merchants, and others, and insisted that they had to limit southern power to promote that welfare.

The pragmatic approach apparently worked well. For a brief time it appeared as if a significant new issue had developed as many Northerners responded favorably to the Provisoist appeal. There were some very excited debates in Congress and, in 1848, a Free Soil party, embodying the anti-slavery extension ideology in its platform (Source 14), entered the electoral lists and received over 300,000 votes in the northern states. Southern leaders also responded to the Provisoist threat by seeking to arouse their section to the growing challenge to their way of life. Several of them attempted to form a sectional political coalition, supported by both southern Whigs and Democrats, united despite their differences on other subjects, in defense of southern institutions. It was this movement that prompted Howell Cobb's affirmation of the national Democratic party in Congress (see Source 2). Others in both sections responded as Cobb had, indicating that, despite all of the agitation, the slavery question had not grown powerful enough to override all other matters dividing the electorate. Most Northerners, including many professed anti-slavery extensionists, supported their traditional parties for traditional reasons. The Whig, Zachary Taylor, a Louisiana slaveholder, won the election with the support of such northern Whigs as Abraham Lincoln of Illinois. There was, it is true, a renewed outbreak of sectional strife after the election as Congress fought over the terms of California's admission into the Union. But even though the debates were quite savage, it was possible for the leaders of the old parties to push through a territorial compromise, despite the opposition of sectionalists, and secure, with some difficulty, the acquiescence of the voters of both sections to the proposals. Finally, to cap it off, both parties declared in their platforms that with the Compromise of 1850, Congress had spoken its final word on slavery and the nation's representatives would neither raise nor discuss the issue further (Source 15). For the moment the finality formula stilled all but a few recalcitrants in both sections.

The Compromise of 1850, however, was not the end of the slavery issue. The nation's continued growth precluded its demise as different sectional interests once again clashed in the territories. In 1854, Senator Stephen A. Douglas moved to extend territorial status to the people of Kansas. Under pressure from southern leaders in the Senate, Douglas included in the bill a provision explicitly repealing the Missouri Compromise line which, for over 30 years, had forbidden the introduction of slavery into the area where Kansas lay. Douglas's action provoked the anti-slavery expansionists all over again, as it confirmed to them that the aggressive southern states would never hesitate to fulfill their hunger for land and power and that northern interests would always be hurt in the process. In a fiery Senate speech in 1854, Salmon P. Chase reawakened the spirit of a few years before (Source 16). The South, he charged, had shattered the calm and torpor of the finality era and had proven once and for all that it would neither keep its bargains nor share the nation's landed wealth with anyone else. The only means of containing southern aggression was for the northern people to wield sufficient political power to prevent further southern hostile actions. Neither of the old parties would or could do this: the Democrats, the "slavocracy" to their enemies, were the willing and pliant tools of southern aggression; the Whigs were weakened by their need for the support of their slave-holding southern wing. A new political coalition, untainted by weaseling Compromise sentiment and by dependence upon southern support, could build up the necessary northern power.

Northern response to the Kansas-Nebraska bill approached all that Chase and his cohorts could have desired. The bitterness of the 1846-1850 period erupted all over again as, in the northern states, hundreds of "Anti-Nebraska" spokesmen attacked the South, Douglas, and the Democratic party. Enough Anti-Nebraska candidates won election to local, state, and congressional offices in 1854 and 1855 to prevent any moves to quiet the North. Southern leaders similarly reawakened the old fears of northern aggression on southern interests. Perhaps the situation would have quieted down as it had in 1850 with the completion of congressional action and a subsequent public acceptance of the *fait accompli*, despite the provocative propaganda efforts in both sections. But this time a running sore remained open. Kansas was on the border of settled areas, quite accessible to people from both free and slave states. Furthermore, after the fight over its organization and the subsequent bitterness, the territory had become a symbol which groups in both sections determined to control. Kansas became the center of a bitter and often deadly conflict as Northerners and Southerners migrated into the area, jockeyed for position, confronted one another, armed themselves, and began fighting. As a result, the tense propaganda duel already under way was worsened as "Bleeding Kansas" helped further polarize political sentiment along sectional lines. Perhaps the most significant and dramatic of the propaganda efforts was Senator Charles Sumner's speech in 1856, "The Crime Against Kansas" (Source 17), which arraigned in severe tones the bloodstained drive for power of the slaveholders. Far more immoderate in tone than the earlier efforts of Wilmot, or the Free Soilers, Sumner's attack provoked such strong reactions that it pushed the process of political change much further along. In passing, Sumner denounced the motives of, and castigated by name, several Senators, among them, Andrew P. Butler of South Carolina. Brooding over what he considered Sumner's insults to his family and to his state, Butler's nephew, Representative Preston Brooks beat Sumner senseless with a cane, driving the latter to a hospital and out of the Senate for three years. Brooks' assault had an effect beyond his anticipations, for it confirmed in many northern minds the truth of Sumner's charges. Southerners were bloodthirsty, aggressive men who would stop at nothing to achieve what they wanted and who would destroy all who stood in their way. Brooks became the "assassin" in northern eyes and was characterized there as the personification of southern depravity (Source 18). Northern reaction grew harsher when Southerners made Brooks a hero who had demonstrated the best way to handle the North's anti-slavery zealots. Virginia's leading newspaper, the *Richmond Enquirer,* led the way in congratulating Brooks and chiding those who deplored the violent action (Source 19).

Sumner's empty seat served during the next few years as the beacon for anti-slavery advocates in Congress and elsewhere. At the same time, continued bloodshed in Kansas, the John Brown raid and Brown's subsequent execution by Virginia authorities, and the mounting passions in Congress and elsewhere, continually thrust the slavery issue into American consciousness. Few advances were made in the quality of the rhetoric used, but many were made in the extremity and violence of the oral warfare. As the virulence grew, some southern leaders became concerned about the possibility of an anti-slavery takeover of the national government on a platform that would ultimately cause the destruction of the South's social system. To prevent this from happening, Representative Reuben Davis of Mississippi said in 1859 (Source 20), the South had to "stand by the Democratic organization, and thereby perpetuate the great doctrine of limitation on the powers of the federal government, and the absolute right of the States to legislate alone upon subjects which concern their domestic and civil rights." But to other southern leaders, Democratic victory was not enough. They also wanted to ensure that the party's stand on slavery in the territories conformed with the South's best interests. They were willing to support the party as their only hope for protection, but the party's victory had to mean a true alternative to Republican assaults on their interests.

For years southern leaders had demanded that the federal government not intervene with slavery, calling the latter a local institution over which Congress had no legislative control even in the territories. They had chafed under such congressional actions as the Missouri Compromise restrictions and had welcomed their removal. They had also accepted some degree of popular sovereignty as better than congressional legislation. Since 1854, however, many of the Southerners had grown increasingly disturbed about popular sovereignty. Stephen A. Douglas's interpretations of territorial legislative power and the fighting in Kansas, where a hostile Northern majority was building up, led southern leaders to believe that popular sovereignty was an inadequate safeguard for their interests. If territorial legislatures could pass hostile legislation, as Douglas claimed, slavery would be shut out of the territories despite its theoretical right to exist there. Therefore, southern leaders made a new demand of the Democratic party. It was, they said, the constitutional duty of the federal government to go beyond a laissez-faire policy on slavery in the territories, and to intervene actively to protect slave property as it did all other personal property there. The territorial legislature, they said, could not infringe on this federal power by limiting slave property in any way. "We want," Senator Jefferson Davis told the Senate in 1860, "nothing more than a simple declaration that Negro slaves are property, and we want the recognition of the obligations of the federal government to protect that property like all others; that is all." Only then would the South's rights be fully guaranteed. Davis framed these demands in a series of congressional resolutions which were hotly debated in Congress, and whose substance was later included in the platform of the Breckinridge Democrats in 1860 (Source 21). At the same time, the Republicans explicitly challenged the southern demands for federal protection for slavery as a "dangerous political heresy" "subversive of the peace and harmony of the country." Such demands, the Republicans claimed, in their 1860 platform, only proved the Democratic party's "measureless subserviency to the exactions of the sectional interest." The fight over the South's demands in the Democratic national convention of 1860, and the Republican response to them, climaxed the series of events which had brought slavery to a position of political prominence in the years before Lincoln's election.

Despite the rising relevance of slavery in American politics, it was never the sole or overriding issue for everyone in the American electorate, even in 1860. Horace Greeley sadly wrote in 1856 that "it is beaten into my bones that the American people are not yet anti-slavery. . . ." Four years later he still felt that the "country . . . will only swallow a little Anti-Slavery in a great deal of sweetening. An Anti-Slavery man per se cannot be elected; but a Tariff, River-and-Harbor, Pacific Railroad, Free Homestead man, *may* succeed *although* he is Anti-Slavery. . . ." There is much evidence indicating the accuracy of Greeley's observations. Certainly, in addition to cultural tensions, and slavery differences, economic matters also played a major role in the complex of issues producing the political changes of the era.

V

In the years between 1840 and 1860, disagreements over the role of the federal government in economic affairs seriously affected the Democratic party by causing important defections to the emerging Republican coalition. These disagreements were rooted in the demands of certain groups for federal aid to promote their economic development. As the depression following the Panic of 1837 waned in the early 1840's, American economic growth sharply spurted forward. A commercial agriculture based on wheat and livestock production grew rapidly in the Ohio-Mississippi-Great Lakes area as one major aspect of this development. The region's producers sent their goods in all directions: southward to the cotton states, eastward to the rising towns of the Atlantic seaboard; and, increasingly, as production spiraled upward, to the European market. By 1846, an Illinois Senator claimed that the wheat produced in only ten counties of his home state could feed the entire domestic market and called, therefore, for rapid development of the foreign markets needed to continue the western boom.

This economic development was, of course, not achieved without some severely limiting problems for the western entrepreneur. One of these concerned land disposal. The federal government owned most of the land in the developing areas and, traditionally, had charged high prices for it. This, coupled with the lack of extensive credit privileges, prevented many people from taking advantage of the available land. As western economic opportunities grew, articulate voices began to demand a more liberal land policy to stimulate further settlement and growth in the region. In the 1830's and 1840's many advances were made in liberalizing land policy through the introduction of price graduation and the right of pre-emption. But many thought this was still not enough to meet the requirements of the booming western economy. Senator Andrew Johnson, therefore, led a bloc of Westerners who pressed for a federal homestead policy throughout the 1850's, which would have made a block of land available at minimum cost to anyone who would settle and work the plot. His defense of the homestead ideal in the Senate, in May, 1858 (Source 22), although occurring late in the period, contained a strong manifestation of the Westerners' vision of economic development based on land accessibility. There were thousands of potential settlers of the public lands, Johnson said, hamstrung and condemned to poverty only by prices higher than most could afford. If these people could buy the land available at minimum rates, it would be quickly absorbed and cultivated. Furthermore, their industry would promote not only their own well-being but also that of the thousands of others in transportation, manufacturing, and the other services necessary to provide necessities for the settlers on the land. A simple federal promotional policy, for which there was ample constitutional provision, he concluded, would have effects far beyond its immediate application in abetting the prosperity of the entire nation.

Another limitation on rapid economic development was the lack of adequate transportation facilities to carry the products of the newly developing regions of the country. The West's navigable waterways, for example, flowed southward to New Orleans, the traditional entrepot for western goods. With the expansion of the region, however, those river channels were insufficient in size and too limited in direction. The Erie Canal had partially broken the mountain barrier to the East but, for the fullest realization of the West's economic potential, the Great Lakes and its ports had to be developed further, the river channels into the Lakes widened and kept free of debris, and more roads, canals, and railroads built. Efforts to build the necessary network had begun in the 1830's but, unfortunately, the depression had exhausted the resources of the states and the private groups who had financed the development before 1837. The federal government appeared to be the only alternative agency capable of extending the necessary funds. Western leaders, faced with the growing constituent pressures, insisted that the federal government step in and expend what was necessary to meet western needs. In November, 1845, a convention met at Memphis, Tennessee, to consider the problems of western economic growth. Their "Memorial," drafted by John C. Calhoun of South Carolina, listed their requirements and strongly argued for an increased federal role in economic expansion (Source 23). Claiming that the improvements they called for were truly national and beneficial to the entire country, the memorialists asked Congress to finance the construction of western carrying facilities, from rivers to railroads.

The demands of the land-hungry and the improvements-conscious were typical of the pressures exerted on Congress and the Executive in the name of economic growth from the middle 1840's onward. Unfortunately the Westerners were hamstrung by the attitude and actions of the party in power. In 1846, Congress passed a wide-ranging rivers and harbors improvement bill which went a long way toward meeting western demands. But the Democratic President, James K. Polk, not only vetoed the bill, but also drafted a long, denunciatory message against the economic extravagance of any such programs (Source 24). Strongly suggesting that such federal aid was unconstitutional, Polk reaffirmed the traditional position of the Democratic party of opposition to excessive federal expenditures. When enough Democrats held their ranks together in Congress under the prodding of the party whips to prevent repassage of the bill over Polk's veto, the cries from western spokesmen, particularly Democrats, were long, loud, and anguished. The Columbus *Ohio Statesman,* the leading Democratic newspaper in that state, bitterly denounced Polk's treachery (Source 25) in the most violently vituperative terms. Other western newspapers, legislators, and spokesmen, were similarly unsparing in their condemnation of Polk's action. They claimed that his actions would fatally injure western interests at the most crucial moment of that region's growth. In Congress, the western Democratic representatives, bitterly aware that the issue of federal aid would remain alive and grow more potent as the economic expansion of the area continued, realized that they had to do something to relieve the pressures and frustrations caused by Polk's actions or lose popular support. But where could they turn? They were still strong supporters of most Democratic policies, they were loyal to their party leaders, and they loathed the Whig organization, despite the latter's traditional support for the very federal aid the West now sought. For the moment, therefore, they remained rooted to their party despite its action. Nevertheless, the activity of the summer of 1846 had produced the outlines of a potential political revolt.

The basic problem was, as in the case of the immigrant danger and slavery extension, that no matter what anyone desired, the issue of economic expansion and its needs remained highly relevant to many Americans. At Chicago, in 1847, an example of this continuing involvement was demonstrated. Another Rivers and Harbors Convention met and became a giant protest meeting against Polk's action and the attitude of the Democratic party in general. Many Democrats attended despite that, and helped pass a series of resolutions explicitly challenging Polk's reasoning of the year before. The ninth resolution (Source 26) reaffirmed, in summary fashion, their position: western commerce needed federal aid; the problem was national, neither local nor sectional; the federal government had the constitutional power to act—and should.

The Chicago meeting was loud, tumultuous, and widely hailed in the West. But it had little immediate effect. In the succeeding years other Democratic presidents repeated Polk's actions, and not only in the case of Rivers and Harbors. In 1854, President Pierce vetoed another internal improvements bill; so did Buchanan several years afterwards (in February, 1860). Buchanan also vetoed a homestead bill which Congress, after much struggle, finally passed in 1859. Buchanan's homestead veto message (Source 27) went far beyond Polk's in foreclosing any change in Democratic policy on economic affairs, by his wide-ranging compilation of reasons against federal expansiveness in economic development. Not only was such aid unconstitutional, Buchanan said, but it was unequal in application, unfair to portions of the population, disastrously destructive of federal revenue, and demoralizing of the "noble spirit of independence" of the American people. Buchanan built part of his justification for the veto of homesteadism on the reasoning he and Polk had used in earlier vetoes of the rivers and harbors bills. Despite the differences in their subject matter, Buchanan saw the two bills as related parts of a common drive for what he called "extravagant legislation" involving "wild schemes of expenditures."

The continued Democratic opposition to an expanded federal role in economic development was matched in the same period by the party's dilatoriness in areas where the leaders believed the government could play some role. Although, as a prime example, the party generally supported the construction of a Pacific railroad, little was accomplished by party leaders due to disagreements over routes, priorities, and financing. Some development bills did occasionally pass through Congress, but only after much struggle against Democratic hostility or indifference. Coupled with their repeated pronouncements against unconstitutional, uneconomic, not to say immoral, federal expenditures, the Democrats' hostility and failure to act confirmed to many in the underdeveloped regions of the country, the absolute necessity for ending Democratic control of the national government.

The Democratic party leaders were well aware of the growing opposition to their policies. They could do little about it, however, since very much like their adversaries, they were responding directly to groups in the party whose conception of correct policy included limited federal aid for internal improvements, no homesteads, and the building of a Pacific railroad only after certain conditions had been met. Their program was as coherent to them as the internal improvements and homestead policies were to the Westerners. The important thing, however, was that the whole controversy, gleefully abetted by the Whig and then the Republican propaganda media, intensified the strains between the western Democrats and their party. As these strains grew, more and more of the economic rebels considered drastic action up to and even including abandoning their party, if necessary to acquire the desired support. A colloquy on the floor of the House of Representatives, in the wake of the Pierce veto of 1854, revealed the increased attractiveness of this idea, so foreign to Howell Cobb a few short years before. There was no more stalwart Democrat than William Richardson of Illinois, but by 1854 he was ready to assert that if western economic interests could not be served in any other way, he would readily join with Whigs, Free-Soilers, and anyone else willing to help push those interests no matter how tainted they might be on other issues (Source 28). The bitterness of continued western economic frustration was producing the formerly unthinkable: extreme disenchantment with one's party.

Even more strained than Richardson's coalitionist position was the reaction of Representative James M. Cavanaugh of Minnesota in response to the failure of so many Democrats to support the homestead bill (Source 29). Once again, Cavanaugh expostulated, the interests of his constituents had been ill served by his party. It was, to his chagrin, the Republican members who had toed the mark with him in the advancement of liberal land policy. His party's failures were enough now, despite the strength of his inherited Democracy, to make him "falter and hesitate" in his devotion. No more clearly worded warning could have emanated from the distressed western Democrats against their party's role in economic legislation. Whatever the real economic effects of Democratic policy on western growth, the point was that many people there, including large numbers of Democrats, had come to believe that the party's continued negativism was destructive of their economic well-being.

The opponents of the Democrats did not let the opportunity presented by these economic tensions pass unnoticed. First the Whigs, then their Republican successors, wooed the Democrats with increasing fervor. The latter most pointedly reiterated that the Democratic party with its dominant financially conservative wing would never meet the West's requirements in economic legislation. The only solution was for the West's leaders to seek a new and friendlier political coalition. The Republicans went well beyond vague rhetorical exhortations. Their national platform in 1860 (Source 30) included planks encompassing every one of the issues which had been a source of internal Democratic tensions over economic development. Building on their own Whig antecedents, with that party's support for expansive federal activity, the Republicans issued ringing declarations in favor of free homesteads, federal aid for rivers and harbors and the construction of a Pacific railroad. To the western Democrats who had carried the words of Polk's original veto as a burning cross for almost fifteen years, the promises were a powerful incentive to change party affiliation, as hard as that may once have been to any one of them.

As in the case of the cultural and slavery issues, the economic factor grew increasingly salient in the two decades before 1860 in response to the rapid expansion and development of the United States. The importance of the role of economic interests in causing political change grew in direct proportion to the failure of the traditional party structure to meet the new requirements of the age. As veto, negative vote, and failure to act followed one another in rapid succession, and the waterways of the West grew less able to cope with economic expansion, a group of Democrats saw the necessity of striking out into new political channels for relief. We do not know how many western Democrats felt the frustrations strongly enough to overcome other objections to changing political direction; certainly many of them, including the champion of free homesteads, Andrew Johnson, maintained their Democratic ties, preferring that association, for whatever complex of reasons, to joining the anti-Democratic group forming in the 1850's. Others were repelled, strikingly enough, by other aspects of the Republican economic program, the high tariff for example. But certainly the Republican efforts to win over these people, and the growth of Republican sentiment in western areas, suggest that, as in the other cases discussed here, economic differences had some effect in promoting the political transformation under way.

VI

By the middle 1850's, political issues rooted in slavery, economics, and cultural tensions had become more important to many Americans than many of the former differences separating Whigs from Democrats. Still needed, however, to complete the process of political change, were organizational efforts, amelioration of potential internal conflicts, the assignment of issue priorities, and the development of a campaign strategy, all necessary to forge different groups into a successful coalition. The anti-Democratic groups disagreed among themselves as to which issues were most important, to be pushed first, and which could be temporarily put aside; whether some ideas should be advocated at all or dropped completely; and what the proper legislative solutions really were for any of them. There were, among the potential Republicans, many areas of common ground but perhaps also, as many possibilities of internal conflict.

In early 1854 meetings were held in such places as Ripon, Wisconsin, and Jackson, Michigan, in response to Congressional action on the Kansas-Nebraska bill. Later that summer and fall, nominees selected by such meetings ran against incumbent Democratic office-holders, usually under an "Anti-Nebraska" party label, although in some places a few men used the old Jeffersonian name of Republican.

From the first, however, these candidates did not limit their appeals for votes to the single issue of the opening of the Nebraska territory to slavery. They appealed also to disgruntled western Democrats, free-land men, old Whigs with their dreams of positive government power, Liberty party and Free-Soil adherents, nativist Know-Nothings, as well as the reputedly anti-slavery Germans with their significant voting strength in several states. Their appeals were to as wide a range of opinion as possible, a range united only in being anti-Democratic and northern because of its anti-slavery aura.

The Anti-Nebraska candidates were quite successful in their quest for votes in 1854, but then disagreed over what to do with their victory. This disagreement lasted right through the election of 1860, as the Republican leaders sought to orchestrate all of the elements present for the twin purposes of Democratic defeat and the enactment of their wide-ranging legislative program. Everyone was, to some degree, suspicious of everyone else. The Democratic element, men like Preston King of New York and John Wentworth of Illinois, were loath to leave the party of their fathers, no matter what its sins, to join a pack of ex-Whigs and be submerged by them. Wentworth, fervently anti-slavery, and also one of the leaders of the internal-improvements Democrats, who had revolted against President Polk, was in 1856 still hesitating to act with the Republican leaders, Whigs "of Know-Nothing and Maine Law proclivities." Whig stalwarts such as Edward Bates of Missouri and Abraham Lincoln also found it difficult to give up traditional ties, even though so many Whigs had drifted off into Know-Nothingism and Republicanism, and the party itself, left behind by the pull of new issues, was all but moribund.

Beyond these personal suspicions and hangovers of partisan prejudices were other deep-seated tensions among those who might be Republicans. Nativist groups were wary of Anti-Nebraska appeals to the Germans, while the Germans were unhappy about the move of the Know-Nothings into the Republican coalition. A German immigrant, now living in Michigan, complained that "our choice in politics leaves much to be desired, slavery on one side, the temperance humbug on the other." Moderate anti-slavery extensionists distrusted the radical abolitionists and Free-Soilers. The latter were similarly suspicious of the moderates. Low-tariff Democrats and high-tariff Whigs were uneasy in each other's company. Temperance men were quick to note any slight to their pet issue. As a result, Republican leaders were constantly beset with the problems of welding together what must often have appeared to be a conglomeration of antipathies. They were never completely successful. Some would-be Republicans never abandoned the Democrats, other groups remained Whigs or became Constitutional Unionists in 1860. Slowly, however, the Republicans overcame their divisions and forged enough groups together into a coalition of some substantial unity. Their leaders played up the issues that held them together: the frustrations and unhappiness caused each group by continuing Democratic policies. They played down or ignored areas of disagreement and sought to prevent any party group from stepping on the toes of another. Abraham Lincoln's unhappy letter to Schuyler Colfax, an Indiana Republican, underscores the difficulties faced by the leaders confronted by the potentially baneful effects for the party if nativist-Republican policies in Massachusetts drove midwestern Germans into the arms of the Democrats (Source 31). The reaction of the Germans to their new companions, and the bitter struggle to keep the former tied to the party in the face of nativist activity, were recounted in the memoirs of the Illinois Republican, Gustave Koerner (Source 32).

Nor were the internal problems rising out of cultural conflicts the only source of trouble for the Republicans. Several moderately anti-slavery groups within the party were upset by the prominence of such men as William Seward of New York, who, more than anyone except Charles Sumner, symbolized an extremist anti-slavery position in this period. In 1859, therefore, Seward, to allay such fears, sought to create a new image of himself and of the party. The advocate of the higher law became a reasonable moderate before the Senate (Source 33).

The Republican efforts were aided by the context of the times: the economic downturn after 1857, which further pointed up the need for federal support for economic development; the unending battle in Kansas, as well as other incidents involving slavery; the continued demonstration of the need for reforms to curb the evils of unrestricted immigration. In 1856, two years after their first steps together, the Republicans won a substantial majority in all but five northern states. By 1860, they won the Presidency and Congress on a platform which was a model of moderation and proper appeal, while at the same time it embraced the range of interests that had brought them together, but also underplayed the potential areas of division. The selection of their candidate in the latter year reflected the problems confronting the party and, also, the leaders' ability to solve them. They forsook Seward, with his extremist aura, and turned away from Edward Bates, conservative on slavery but a former Know-Nothing. Instead they chose the moderate anti-slavery extensionist, Abraham Lincoln, who had directly opposed Douglas on the question of Democratic policies in Kansas, who had represented his state at the great Chicago Rivers and Harbors Convention, and whom the Illinois Germans trusted. Lincoln's combination of qualities represented the best of what the Republicans were stressing in their drive for victory. Although they did not get everyone they wanted—German Catholics for one, voted Democratic —they did get enough to win.

The Democratic situation had not been static while the Republicans forged their coalition. They suffered, as we have seen, some important defections from their ranks. Still, however, despite their financial conservatism, indifference to slavery, and other deficiencies, they maintained the loyalty of many Northerners. The Irish and German Catholic rank and file rejected the Republican identification with temperance and nativism. Many of the traditional Democrats in the West and North, not significantly affected by the pressures splitting the party, continued to stress the issues that had made and kept them Democrats. Still, as the Republicans continually emphasized, Democratic leadership, sources of voting strength, and policies revealed an increasing southern aura to that party. That sectional cast was stimulated further because so many former southern Whigs joined the Democrats in the 1850's in defense of sectional rights.

For many years southern politics had been as divided as that of the rest of the country. The same issues dividing national politics into Whig and Democratic components were also important in the slave states. This internal political division never wholly disappeared from the ante-bellum South. As late as 1860, many of the southern Whigs still fought against Democratic policies. But the onrush of the slavery issue, the rise of the Republicans, and the resulting fears of social upheaval brought many southern Whigs into the Democratic party. As Henry Hilliard, former Whig congressman from Alabama recalled in his memoirs, "the formidable display of strength by the anti-slavery party of the North made it plain that the interests of the Southern people demanded that any differences of sentiment as to other questions should be subordinated to resistance to this threatened aggression upon our rights." His letter to the national Whig organ, the *National Intelligencer* in 1857 (Source 34) was a fervent call to his fellow Whigs to forsake all former differences and join him in moving into the Democratic party. Many of these new Democrats never stopped disagreeing with the policies of their new party, outside of the matter of slavery, and, as in the case of the Republicans, there were many tensions within the party. But, as was also the case with the Republicans, concentration on the proper combination of issues kept the Whigs in their new political home.

The race issue was to become a potent and everlasting part of southern politics, and its intense growth in the 1850's was the last stage in the transformation of prewar American politics, for the Southerners did not stop with the forging of their own unity. They also tried, with great effort and determination, to impose their sectional viewpoint and program on the Democratic party. Distrustful of popular sovereignty, they tried to commit the national Democracy to the policy of federal protection of slavery in the territories. Although the northern Democrats resisted this bitterly as a suicidal demand, the damage was done. The party split apart in its national convention in 1860 and then washed its dirty linen in public. Such cranky exchanges over territories, disloyalty, and plighted faith, as that between Senators Pugh, Benjamin, and Wigfall (Source 35), only worsened the situation for the party as a national force. Its inability to function effectively, shorn of its southern wing, and to escape thereby its aura of subservience to the slavery interest was underlined. Despite their northern supporters, the charge was confirmed that the Democrats were pliable tools of the slave power who would remain ever unresponsive to the sources of northern discontent.

VII

In the two decades between 1840 and 1860, the national political synthesis rooted in the conflicts of the 1820's and 1830's gave way before the rising importance of issues which, although present in the earlier period, did not then have the intensity they developed after 1840. And as a new political synthesis developed, based on cultural issues, economic frustrations, and slavery extension, the basic nature of American political life shifted significantly. As in all transformations, much of the old structure remained as part of the new. There was still a two party system. The Democrats received about the same share of the popular vote, 47 per cent in 1860 and afterwards, as they had averaged between 1840 and 1856. Many of the same issues were discussed in 1860 as in 1840. Nevertheless, this was a period of major realignment of the voting groups supporting each party coalition. Many former Democrats, as we have seen, joined the Republicans in response to their changing perception of their needs, goals, and the actions of the groups around them. On the other side, for similar reasons, some former Whig groups had become Democrats. The result was that in the crucial presidential election just before the Civil War a new political structure was in the process of gaining control of the American political scene.

The outstanding characteristic of the political system of 1840 had been its nationality. Although sectional differences and local considerations had played some role in the earlier period, the thrust of politics was nonsectional in nature. Appeals for votes were to a national constituency; flamingly sectional appeals led only to defeat. By 1860, however, this nationality had dramatically disappeared. A northern political coalition won control of the government on a platform frankly appealing to northern groups alone. Although the Democrats were never as thoroughly sectionalized as their opponents, by the very nature of the latter's efforts they were thrust into a southern mold in the public mind. They continued to win victories in some northern areas, but such successes did not alter the fact that their leadership, its program, and much of its popular support appeared increasingly to be oriented toward the South. The events of 1860-1877 only confirmed what had occurred before 1860. A solid South emerged on one hand, and, on the other, the Republicans centered their appeal on the North. The political pattern established would not be altered for many years to come. Only with urbanization, the rise of the immigrant groups in the North to power after 1920, the economic dislocation of the 1930's, and the emergence of the Negro as a major political force, would there be a significant move back toward the national politics of the era before the Civil War.

What was the key determinant of this political transformation? Although many historians have described the slavery problem as the overriding issue of the time, it is probably true that no one factor was necessarily more significant in the total picture than any other. The fight over slavery caused some major shifts of voting groups, but so did the cultural tensions and the economic problems. As we have seen, different people perceive issues with different intensities of interest, assign them different priorities of importance, and are affected by them in different ways. There are many times when one issue overrides all of the others in the political complex. But this period was not one of them. Rather, each of the matters discussed here: economic needs, ethnocultural differences, and slavery, all played some role, individually, in combination, and with varying degrees of strength from group to group and locale to locale, to cause the political shifts of the period after 1840. The important fact about the whole period was that all of these issues operated powerfully enough to lead to the emergence of the Republican party on one hand, and a shifting focus on the part of the Democrats on the other, two most significant consequences for the political structure of the United States.

JOEL H. SILBEY

Cornell University

The Grounds of Difference between the Contending Parties

Horace Greeley

Two great rival hosts now divide the American People, and by their struggles for ascendancy agitate, and at intervals, convulse the Nation. Each is probably right in many of the principles which it affirms; each is doubtless wrong in some of the acts which it commits or tolerates, and in the extremes to which its views are sometimes pushed. Each embodies a share of the wisdom and folly, honesty and knavery, virtue and vice, which chequer human life. Each numbers in its ranks stern and lofty patriots, who have no thought but for their country's good; each has also its self-seeking demagogues, who regard mainly their own advantage. He who deems his own party all good, and his opponents wrong [in] every way, may be an excellent partisan, but not a very discerning and impartial citizen. Yet, while many faults and many virtues are common to both and to all parties, there are certain great leading characteristics which at this time draw a broad and distinct line of demarkation between them. These characteristics we shall here endeavor to exhibit.

I. The first is generic or fundamental, influencing and shaping all the others. It is the cardinal conviction of those known as Whigs ("Democratic" or "Federal" Whigs, as you please), that Government need not and should not be an institution of purely negative, repressive usefulness and value, but that it should exert a beneficent, paternal, fostering influence upon the Industry and Prosperity of the People. It affirms that the People can never expect too much from the Government, when they expect the interest of the Government and the interest of the People are or should be identical, and ought never to be regarded as diverse, and, in short, that Government was founded, and

The Whig Almanac for 1843 (New York, 1843), pp. 29-30.

is supported, in order that it may promote the welfare and happiness of the People by every means legitimately within its power. The opposite party (whether termed "Democrats," as they claim to be, or "Loco-Focos," as is less vague and more pertinent) assume that "the world is governed too much"; that Government has properly nothing to do with the concerns of the People, except to protect them from external or internal aggression; that when it has provided fully to repel invasion from without, and to punish crime within the Nation, it has performed its whole duty, and, should it attempt any thing farther, would be morally certain to do more harm than good. Such is substantially the radical difference between the Whigs and Loco-Focos of this country.

II. The question of Protection to Home Industry is the first in importance of those necessarily dividing the two parties, in view of the difference above stated. The Whig doctrine affirms that Government ought to protect and cherish the Industry of the Country to the fullest extent, as a matter of legitimate and necessary concern; and that the People have a *right* to look to it for all the aid within its power. Loco-Focoism, on the other hand, insists that Protection is at once usurpation and folly; that Industry should look out for itself; and that Government neither can nor should do anything in its behalf, in any contingency. There are individuals in the Whig party opposed to the policy of Protection, as there are in the Loco-Foco who favor that policy; but the question no less clearly involves the radical difference between the two parties.

III. Akin to this is the Currency question. The Whigs maintain that it is the duty of the Government to provide, and that the necessities of the People demand, a National Circulating Medium of uniform soundness and value, circulating from one end of the Union to the other without discount and without cavil, being always redeemed in specie, and everywhere received by the Treasury in all payments thereto. They hold it impossible that coin alone shall perform this service, because of its weight, its bulk, and the difficulty and cost of its transmission; while they insist that no paper not possessing a National character, or not redeemable on demand in specie, can ever be expected to do it. The great advantages of such a Circulating Medium as the country enjoyed from 1824 to 1836, and as the Whigs hope to restore, must be evident to all. Suppose that the annual exchanges of products between different sections of the Union, so remote as not to possess a uniform local Currency, now amount to Five Hundred Millions per annum (which it probably exceeds), and that the average cost of difference of Exchange, discount on Bank notes, &c., is but four per cent. on the amount; here, in the absence of a National Currency, is an annual Tax of Twenty Millions per annum levied on the Productive Industry of the Country for nothing, or to support an army of Brokers, Traveling Agents, &c., who would otherwise be employed in useful industry. It is the same as though one twenty-fifth of all the merchantable Produce and Goods of the Country were annually sunk to the bottom of the Sea. Therefore, say the Whigs, object as you may to the powers or management of this Bank, or that Fiscal Agency, but do not deprive the Country utterly of great advantages which it once enjoyed and may well enjoy again. To say that we ought not to have a National Currency because Nick Biddle was a rascal, or his Bank corruptly managed, is to trifle with the good sense of the Country. Nobody so acts on such considerations in his own personal matters. If there were defects or perverted powers in a former institution, experience should teach us how to amend them; but to argue thence that we should have none, is like insisting that the explosion of a boiler should put an end to Steam navigation. On all this subject, the Loco-Foco doctrine is the opposite of the Whig, and the instances of individual dissent are on either side very few.

IV. On Internal Improvement, the fundamental principles of the two parties come again in contact. The Whigs maintain that the primary consideration which should govern the commencement and prosecution of Internal Improvements is the largest degree of benefit to the whole People, and that whenever a Canal or Railroad is clearly proved to be eminently calculated to advance the interests of the community, by cheapening transportation, increasing production, and developing resources which would else lie dormant—and all this to an extent vastly surpassing the cost of the work—then it would be politic and just to construct it, if within the ability of the community, although it might not at first pay the interest on the outlay. The Whig party generally look with favor upon works of Internal Improvement, regarding them as calculated and intended to give employment to Labor, secure a market to Produce, and contribute generally and vastly to the physical improvement of the country, and its advancement in Arts, Civilization, and Morality. Loco-Focoism, on the contrary, although its disciples have in other times commenced their full share of

unprofitable and burdensome, because uncompleted works, regards
with jealousy the prosecution of Public Works, and sees in them only
the preludes to taxation, bankruptcy, and ruin. Its estimate of the
utility and policy of a proposed Canal or Railroad is based on the pre-
sumption that it will or will not pay readily a good interest on the cost
of its construction; unheeding the advantages which may flow from it
through other channels than its tollhouses. But Loco-Focoism in practice is every day becoming more and more assimilated to what we have
seen that it is in principle—hostile to any action of the Government
designed to promote affirmatively the welfare of the People. In New
Hampshire, the party has taken decided ground, not only against any
direct aid to Railroads by the State, but also against granting permission
to companies to take the lands over which their Roads must pass at an
impartial valuation. This refusal is fatal to *any* prosecution of Improvement. No Company will undertake a work which may be stopped
midway by a demand of ten thousand dollars a foot for land they must
pass over. But here and everywhere, those who are the genuine disciples of this faith, being alike hostile to the involving States or Communities in Public Works, and at the same time hostile to the incor-
poration of Companies with capital and powers adequate to their construction, in effect oppose and deny all the means by which such
works can be carried forward, since individual capital, enterprise, and
powers, can rarely if ever be equal to the construction of works of the
highest public utility. Hence Internal Improvement and Loco-Focoism
are at deadly variance; they can co-exist only through gross inconsist-
ency on the part of those professing the latter.

V. Again, there occurs a radical difference on the subject of the
Public Lands. Loco-Focoism asserts, that whatever may be realized
upon the sale of these Lands shall go into the Federal Treasury, and
be used to defray the ordinary and current expenses of the Government.
But the Whigs insist that these Lands are the common property of all
the *States* of the Union; that they were expressly so ceded by the few
States in whom the title was vested at the close of the Revolution; and
that the express condition was that their proceeds were to aid first in
extinguishing the Revolutionary debt, and then to belong to the States
—the Federal Union not having then been formed. That debt being
now extinguished, the Whigs contend that the Land Proceeds should
be fairly and equally distributed to the several States, to be by them
applied to purposes of Education and Internal Improvement, so that

they shall annually add to the enduring wealth of the country, and to the intellectual and physical advantages enjoyed by our People. They urge that the proceeds of this vast and precious Public Domain—the noblest patrimony ever yet inherited by any People—ought not to be frittered away or eaten up from year to year like the estate of a prodigal, but should be husbanded and preserved with care, in such manner that future generations shall not reproach us with having squandered what was justly theirs, and left them penniless. To these are added many weighty considerations connected with the danger of an ultimate alienation of this great domain from the whole People to the sole use and benefit of the States which contain them, and of the depreciation of the value of lands in the Old States through a graduation or reduction of the price, &c. All these considerations are lost upon Loco-Focoism, which insists that the Land Proceeds shall be thrown into the Treasury and expended like any other Revenue of the Federal Government. On this point also the fundamental difference between the parties respecting the nature and true ends of Government is clearly manifested.

Such are some of the most important questions at issue between the two great parties which divide the Country. We have aimed to state them temperately, fairly, and justly, without resorting to harsh epithets, or invoking blind, unreasoning prejudices. These questions are about to be settled by the judgement and action of the People. Let every man deliberately, calmly assume his position on that side which his understanding shall point out as that of the true principles and best interests of the American Republic.

The Necessity for Party Organization

Howell Cobb

The gentleman from Pennsylvania [Mr. Stewart] . . . has not only attacked the platform upon which the Democratic party professed to stand in the coming contest, but has denounced everything like party organization. He informs us that the time has arrived when party organization should be set aside, and party lines obliterated—when men should be elevated to the highest offices of the Republic irrespective of all party consideration—when the people should be called upon to cast their ballots regardless of the influences of party or the principles of candidates. . . . Whence have originated parties in this country? Who were the fathers of party organization? Look to the history of the best and purest days of the Republic; go back to 1800, when Thomas Jefferson, at the head of the Republican party, and Alexander Hamilton, at the head of the Federal party, arrayed their opposing principles, and the people rallied around their respective standards as their hearts and minds sanctioned the one or the other. During that mighty contest, of principle, which moulded into shape and form the two great parties of the country, what voice was heard proclaiming the heretical sentiment of "no-partyism and no-principles"—the present rallying cry of the Whig party? Think you not, sir, that it would have fallen as a strange sound upon the ears of our Republican fathers, if, in the midst of their anxious and untiring effort to preserve and bear aloft the great principles of constitutional liberty, they had been told, as we are to-day, that they were wrong in organizing a party to carry out their principles, and that their frank and open avowal of them was but a shallow device to delude and deceive the people? Such a suggestion during that memorable period

Speech of Howell Cobb of Georgia, July 1, 1848; *Congressional Globe,* 30th Cong., 1st sess., *Appendix,* pp. 775-77.

would have been frowned down with scorn and indignation by every republican heart in the land. It deserves no other fate today.

What, Mr. Chairman, is party? Is it a mere catchword, used to delude, deceive, and impose upon the honest people of the land? Or is there something in that word, of principle, which commends it to the intelligence and integrity of the country? It is an association of men acting in concert with each other, to carry out great fundamental principles in the administration of Government. Men of the same political faith agree to unite their efforts for the purpose of placing in the responsible offices of the Government those of their fellow-citizens whose opinions and principles accord with their own, in order that their Government may be administered upon those principles which in their judgment will best promote the general interest and prosperity of the country. . . . It enables the people to declare their will in a practical form, and compels a compliance with it on the part of their agents. It carries the beautiful theory of our system into practical operation, and makes our Government, what it ought to be, and what our fathers intended it should be—a Government of the people.

The effort to break down party organization is a blow at the very corner stone of our whole political system. It strikes at the fundamental principle of self-government, and seeks to paralyze the arm of the people by relieving their agents and representatives from all responsibility to them as the source from which all power emanates. . . . We stand here to-day indebted to party organization for all the important measures of national reform and constitutional rights which mark the brilliant administrations of Jefferson, Madison, and Jackson. I need not enumerate them. They are fresh in the recollection of the people. They stand impressed upon the pages of our country's history, and embalmed in the hearts of her republican sons. The true Democrat looks back with pride and pleasure to those glorious triumphs of political truth and justice achieved by his Democratic fathers, under the same time-honored banner that now waves its ample folds over the Democracy of the Union. It affords him the amplest assurances of the justice of his cause and the correctness of his principles, drawing him into closer alliance with his brethren of the same political faith, and stimulating him to renewed efforts in the noble work, commenced by his fathers, consecrated by their wisdom and blessings, and destined, in its ultimate and permanent triumph, to perpetuate to his children and countrymen the inestimable blessings of free government.

We are now called upon to renounce a system from which all these blessings have flown—to disband the Democratic party—to throw our cherished principles to the winds, and blindly to follow the erratic lead of those who have devoted their whole lives to one unceasing warfare upon everything we hold dear and sacred in our political faith. . . .

I now come to party platforms, which seem a favorite theme with my colleague [Mr. Toombs], who has argued the question with his usual ability and ingenuity. What is a party platform? An avowal of principles. Is it anything more? A man is presented to the people of the United States as the candidate for a responsible office: is it right or wrong that the people should know what are his principles? That is the question. If a man is intrusted with the highest power known to the world—the guardianship of the interests of this great people— he is required by the Constitution to recommend measures for the action of Government. The Constitution places in his hand a power to be exercised to protect and guard it, as well as the great rights and interests of the people under it. . . . When freemen are asked to cast their votes for a man, and to repose their confidence in a party, they will not be content to acquiesce in the declaration, that neither the one nor the other have any avowals of principles or opinions for the public eye. The answer given at the polls by an indignant and out-raged people to such effrontery and pretensions will be, "You have no communications for us; we have none for you. . . ." Our candidates and our principles are before the country. The success of the one is the triumph of the other. In addition to them, we offer to the people of the Union the successful administration of the Government under every Democratic President, as the surest guarantee of the continued happiness and prosperity of our country, so long as it is administered upon the sound and wholesome principles of Democratic policy.

A Serious Public Evil

John P. Sanderson

The immense immigration of late years, and the palpable growing influence of the foreign born has become a source of anxiety, and it is not now regarded with great favor by any considerable portion of the native citizens. Many causes have conspired to produce this change of sentiment and feeling in the American people, and to induce a very general conviction, that the present unlimited and unguarded admission of foreigners into this country, is a serious public evil. . . .

Yet, with all these evils flowing from the unguarded admission of foreigners, evils of every class and character, affecting all the relations of life, there is no disposition among the native born Americans to discourage the immigration of moral and industrious Europeans. On the contrary, they rejoice in being able to furnish them an asylum from oppression, and a home in which they may enjoy all the blessings of liberty; but they neither feel nor feign any attachment or regard for the criminals and adventurers who have left their own country for their country's good. They gladly welcome to their country every honest and industrious man in Europe, with this exception, that they do not come to rule America, but to be content to let those rule who are to the manor born. "We do not propose," is the language of a recent address of the American State Council of Georgia, "to shut our doors on the world, but that we continue to be the asylum of the oppressed of all nations. Let the victims of civil and ecclesiastical tyranny come. What we mean to say is, that with our consent they shall not rule the land."

All that is desired of foreigners is to lay aside their national pe-

John P. Sanderson, *Republican Landmarks: The Views and Opinions of American Statesmen on Foreign Immigration* (Philadelphia, 1856), pp. 204-6, 216-17, 219, 229-30, 234, 334-36.

culiarities and prejudices, to deport themselves with becoming modesty and propriety, and, instead of at once mingling in political broils, and attempting to regulate and control public affairs, mind their own private business. No American finds fault with them for remembering the country of their birth. All they would have the foreigner do is to study to become a good and useful citizen, making himself acquainted with the principles of the government, imbibing the spirit and genius of its institutions, assimilating himself to its manners and customs, and, in a word, to fear God and honor the country of his adoption. Alas! there are, however, too many of the immigrants from the Old World who do not thus conduct themselves after their arrival in this country, and hence the prevailing sentiment now extant among the native citizens, in favor of restricting, by law, the power and privileges of aliens to within prudent limits. No such general feeling would probably now exist, had the foreigners been content with a rational exercise of the privileges which are so freely by law conferred upon them; but, instead of enjoying these in that becoming and unassuming manner which would do them most credit, and exerting themselves to the utmost to lay aside their nationality, and assimilate in character, habits, manners and associations with the native born, they have formed clans, and organized into bands, whose misconduct is but the too frequent cause of disorder and tumult in our large towns and cities. Nor is this all. Instead of refraining from participating in political and religious controversy, they have been the most active in introducing it on both subjects. They have not been satisfied with the rights of citizenship and the protection of American laws, but demand office as a right, and even insist upon the political proscription of Americans for resisting their demand. Need we, then, wonder that they have become obnoxious . . . ?

The truth is, the Irish are greatly to blame themselves for the ill-feeling that now exists among the Americans against them, and those of them who are Roman Catholics may thank the foreign priesthood of their church for the distrust with which they and their religion are regarded by so large a number of American Protestants. Irish men have never been favorites with the Anglo-Saxon race, and it is undoubtedly true that the same feeling which has existed for centuries towards them in England, has, in a more modified and less illiberal form, all along pervaded the Anglo-Saxon race in this country; while the dislike to Roman Catholics has grown up into a strong feeling, not so much in consequence of hostility to the Roman Catholic religion, as on account of the bigoted teachings and conduct of its foreign priesthood. . . .

Such, too, is eminently the case with a very large class of the German immigrants. . . . Liberty to them is a vague and indefinite idea, and, under their guardianship, would soon be nothing more nor less than licentiousness. Imbued with the German philosophy of European revolutionary leaders, and filled with new, strange, and bewildering theories of the destiny of man and of human society, they soon find, on their arrival here, that their ideas of universal happiness are not likely to be realized, in the present state of American society, or under the existing form of government, and they become accordingly the advocates for the abolition of both. Denying all imperfection in the nature of man, and finding the Christian religion in the way of their social and political reform, they do not hesitate to assail the religion as well as the government of our revolutionary ancestors. . . . Its members are not a desirable class of people to be invested with the rights of citizenship, until they are more capable of appreciating the principles and structure of our government than they now are. . . .

America for Americans, is a demand not based upon narrow sectarianisms, or mere party predilections. It is no new doctrine; it has been avowed and maintained in all ages, and in all countries, so long as the people remained true to their country, and had a respect for and pride in their nationality; it rests upon the love of home and of country, and involves not only a natural right but a solemn and imperative duty which birth-right alone can impose. . . .

Why, then, should it be deemed illiberal, unkind and unjust in Americans to feel a devotion to their country, and an interest in its institutions which induces a desire on their part to rule America? Have not other free nations claimed and exercised the same prerogative? And was it not only when they became too degenerate and corrupt to do so that they lost their birthright and with it their nationality? Did not Daniel O'Connell raise the talismanic cry among his countrymen, of *Ireland for the Irish?* Yet no one ever charged him on that account as a narrow-minded, illiberal bigot; on the contrary, he was universally extolled as sensible and patriotic, and, in America at least, there was but one response, and that was, that it was but a just and natural claim, which ought not to be denied by Great Britain, that "none but Irishmen should rule Ireland." If the sentiment was correct, and Irishmen in this country all united in expressing it, why should they now find fault with it when applied to America?

The Americans are but discharging a duty they owe to the land of their birth, equally due to the memory of their revolutionary ancestors and to their own posterity, when they set to work to purify the body-politic from disease which threatens destruction to the country, and to the institutions committed to their guardianship by their forefathers. What is the malady that afflicts us?—what the evil they have set about to remedy? In one generation we have attained a growth exceeding that of any other nation; our flag floats in every sea, and is every where honored and respected; while our institutions are the theme of admiration throughout the civilized world; and yet we are obliged to struggle to maintain our distinct nationality at home. Millions of the oppressed in other lands resort hither to enjoy the blessings of freedom, and, in our contact with those who thus seek refuge from tyranny, our system has been inoculated with the decayed matter of the worn out, corrupt and dying systems of the old world, which renders it necessary to purify ourselves and lop off the fungus. And are Americans to be blamed for this? Surely no one can assert the affirmative and satisfactorily maintain it. Say what we will, there exists such an evil in the country. The people know and feel it. The gross abuses of the hospitality extended to those of foreign birth, and the outrageous violations of our laws, and infringements upon our rights, by foreigners coming among us—incited thereto, it must be, with sorrow and shame, confessed, by demagogues and knavish politicians in our own country—has been for a long while an alarming and growing evil in our elections, until at length it has become intolerable.

It is notorious that the grossest frauds have been practiced on our naturalization laws, and that thousands and tens of thousands have every year deposited votes in the ballot box, who could not only not read them, and knew nothing of the nature of the business in which they were engaged, but who had not been six months in the country, and, in many cases, hardly six days. By such influences, by the destruction of ballot boxes, and by forcibly preventing native born citizens from coming to the polls, the foreign element has at times carried the elections in our cities and towns, and thereby controlled States and the Union! The power thus wielded has led to the most disgraceful subserviency to the foreign element on the part of our native demagogues, and wholesale bargaining and traffic has been the result.

It is in the horror and disgust of such a state of things that the American movement has had its origin, and that has given a healthful tone to public sentiment in regard to the evil under which the country has labored. The people have become aroused to the danger, and have accordingly determined to guard against it by placing the power of ruling only into the hands of those in whose devotion to the country they feel they may have confidence.

source 4

Evils of Immigration

Samuel C. Busey

Among the evils incident to immigration, crime and pauperism are not the least important. . . . The census of 1850 shows that, during the year ending June 30, 1850, the number of persons who received "the benefit of the public funds of the different states," was 134,972; of this number there were 68,538 of foreign birth, and 66,434 native Americans. . . .

One in every 32 foreigners is a pauper; whereas, but one in 317 Americans is a pauper; then it follows that the proportion of native and foreign pauperism is one to ten. These calculations . . . show conclusively that the source of pauperism in this country is immigration. This conclusion is confirmed by an examination of the pauper statistics of those countries from whence come the immigrants. The proportion of pauperism to the population of the European countries, varies from 25 to 15 per cent. In the Netherlands, in 1847, one-fifth of the population were paupers; in Great Britain and Wales, in 1848, one in every eight persons was a pauper, and when these facts are

Samuel C. Busey, *Immigration: Its Evils and Consequences* (New York, 1856), pp. 107-9, 117-21, 126.

taken in connection with the policy adopted by foreign countries, of shipping to this country their paupers, it is not at all remarkable that the proportion of paupers among the immigrants should be so large. Immigration is indiscriminate, consequently, it is not surprising that the ratio of pauperism to the foreign population is so great. The cause of immigration to this country, to a very great extent, is pauperism abroad; and pauperism here is the consequence of indiscriminate immigration. . . .

Since 1850, immigration has vastly increased, and with it its attendant evils; and though there are no official estimates of pauperism since that period, there exist sufficient data upon which to venture a calculation. . . . The conclusion is inevitable that there is a necessity for a reformation in the naturalization laws. Pauperism is an evil, a curse, a blight, and immigration is its principal source.

FOREIGN AND NATIVE CRIME

To continue the comparison between the foreign and native population, which has been commenced, the investigation of the subject of crime comes next in order.

The census of 1850 shows that the whole number of persons convicted of crime in the United States, during the year ending June 30, 1850, was 27,000, of which 13,000 were of native, and 14,000 of foreign birth. The foreign exceed the native, 1,000. The relative proportion of foreign and native crime can be determined by comparing these statistics respectively with the foreign and native population, thus:

	Population	Criminals	Proportion of crime
Native population	21,031,569	13,000	1 to 1619
Foreign population	2,240,535	14,000	1 to 154

One out of every 154 foreigners is a criminal, and but one in every 1,619 Americans. The proportion of native and foreign crime, then, is as 1 to 10—one American to ten foreigners.

But another view may be taken of this subject, and in doing so it will be necessary to again call attention to the number of criminals who were convicted by the courts of several States in 1850. In Connecticut, the whole number of convictions was 850; and of these, 545 were natives, and 305 foreigners. In Illinois, the whole number convicted was 316; and of these, 127 were natives, and 189 foreigners. In Maine, the whole number convicted, 744; and of these, 284 were natives, and 460 foreigners. In Massachusetts, the whole number convicted was 7,250; and of these, 3,336 were natives, and 3,884 foreigners. In Missouri, there were 908 convictions; and of these, 242 were natives, and 666 foreigners. In New York, the number of convictions was 10,279; and of these, 3,962 were natives, and 6,317 foreigners. In Pennsylvania, the number of convictions, 857; and of these, 594 were natives, and 293 foreigners. In Vermont, the number convicted, 79; of whom 34 were natives, and 45 foreigners.

By a table published in the Compendium of the Seventh Census, giving the number of convicts in the prisons and penitentiaries of the several States, out of every ten thousand of the population, the proportion of natives and foreigners in the number is as follows:

	Foreign		Native
In Maine	5	to	1
In Kentucky	6	to	1
In Mississippi	5	to	1
In New York	3	to	1
In Tennessee	15	to	2
In Vermont	8	to	1
In South Carolina	28	to	1
In Alabama	50	to	1
In Georgia	6	to	1
In Indiana	4	to	1

. . . If the comparison had been instituted between the native white population and the foreign, which is also white, thus representing the American and European nations, the relative proportion of crime among the two classes would have been greater, and when the fact is taken into consideration, that only the white native and the immigrant or European population are entitled to or ever exercise the rights of citizenship—which is the only just political view of the question, for it is the political power and influence of foreigners which we seek to counteract and destroy—the comparison thus instituted between the two classes of white people would be more just and appropriate, and would more correctly exhibit the evil and danger attendant upon indiscriminate immigration, to the institutions, safety, and welfare of our common country. . . .

From the American Almanac for 1855, the following statistics of conviction are obtained for the year 1854.

State	No. of convictions	Native	Foreign
Rhode Island	174	132	42
New York	702	286	259
New Jersey	119	43	76
Pennsylvania	124	83	41
Pennsylvania	63	40	23
Maryland	142	100	42
Louisiana	379	265	114
Ohio	229	129	100
Indiana	141	97	44

The foreign population in 1850 was about one eighth of the native and free negro. It would seem, then, but natural that the convictions among the native should be eight times as numerous as among the foreign. By an examination of the above table, it will be seen that the foreign convicts average, taking all the States mentioned together, about one half of the number of the native convicts.

These statistics and calculations clearly prove immigration to be the chief source of crime in this country. Besides those who are convicted of crime after their arrival here, there are many criminals transported here by the European governments. Crime and pauperism are both evils, injurious to the character and standing either of a community or a government, and for both of them we are mainly dependent upon immigration.

EFFECT OF FOREIGN PAUPERISM AND CRIME

It has been shown in the foregoing, that in proportion to the native and foreign population, there are ten foreign paupers to one American, and ten foreign criminals to one native. The inevitable conclusion is, that immigration is an evil, and that it is the principal source of crime and pauperism in this country.

In estimating the value of immigration, or the importation of foreigners, these grievous evils demand the serious reflection and mature consideration of every reflecting individual. If viewed as a business transaction—as a mere matter of dollars and cents—it must occur to every individual that the native population must bear the burden of expenses necessary to maintain these paupers, and to bring these offenders against the laws of the country to justice.

The accompanying table exhibits the cost of foreign pauperism in the several States, as shown by the census of 1850.

*A Table showing the Number and Cost of Foreign Paupers
in the several States*

State	Foreign paupers	Cost foreign paupers	Native paupers
Maine	950	$26,600	4,553
N. Hampshire	747	33,577	2,553
Vermont	1,611	52,098	2,043
Massachusetts	9,247	229,759	6,530
Rhode Island	1,445	25,865	1,115
Connecticut	465	23,906	1,872
New York	40,580	553,918	19,275
New Jersey	576	22,407	1,816
Pennsylvania	5,653	113,060	5,898
Delaware	128	3,274	569
Maryland	1,903	30,333	2,591
Virginia	185	5,513	4,933
N. Carolina	18	559	1,913
S. Carolina	329	8,782	1,313
Georgia	58	1,567	978
Florida	12	147	64
Alabama	11	531	352
Mississippi	12	836	248
Louisiana	390	27,318	133
Texas	—	—	7
Tennessee	11	337	994
Arkansas	8	331	97
Kentucky	155	8,431	971
Ohio	609	25,578	1,904
Michigan	541	12,329	649
Indiana	322	25,597	860
Illinois	411	23,217	386
Missouri	1,729	30,963	1,248
Iowa	35	1,786	100
Wisconsin	497	10,998	169
Total	68,538	$1,299,619	66,134

To these amounts must be added the cost of maintaining the county and town paupers, which are separate from the State paupers.

The money thus expended is collected by taxation; and even though the paupers may almost wholly inhabit the cities and towns, yet they are maintained at the expense of the State, the revenues of which are raised or collected by a tax, levied upon property and business. The native population bear the burden of this tax. . . .

From the foregoing the following are the logical deductions:

1. That immigration is the source of crime.
2. That immigration is the source of pauperism.
3. That immigration conduces to disease, disorder, and immorality.
4. It is a tax upon the property and business pursuits of the native. Besides this, they are bought up at elections, and control them, and make riot, bloodshed, and murder.

Formerly, the better class came. The old Scotch merchant and Dutch farmer were clever. They came with their substance, not only to adopt a country, but to help to build it up. But they that come *now* come to *live* upon the country.

It needs no comment. No more potent argument could be urged in favor of the present "American Reformation." Pauperism and crime are the inevitable results of foreign immigration. Yet, to gratify demagogues and unprincipled partisan politicians, must we continue, by Congressional legislation, to encourage the importation of pauperism, crime, and destitution? No national purpose can be promoted, no republican institutions can be sustained, by such a course of policy. Besides the direct result, there are many collateral influences, consequent upon the unrestricted importation of foreigners.

One of the Most Alarming
"Signs of the Times"

William G. Brownlow

The great criminal of the nineteenth century, the PAPAL HIER-
ARCHY, is now on trial before the bar of public opinion, having been
arraigned by the AMERICAN PARTY. You are called on to decide . . .
whether this Criminal, arraigned for treason against God, and hostility
to the human race, deserves the execrations of all honest and patriotic
men, and avenging judgments of a righteous God! In order to decide
this grave question . . . you are to consider the inevitable tendency
of the principles of the Church of Rome—the actual results of these
tendencies as embodied in history. . . .

Popery is deceitful in its character; and the design of this brief
work is, in part, to drag it forward into the light of the middle of the
nineteenth century, to strip the flimsy vizor off its face, and to bring
it, with all its abuses, corruptions, and hypocritical Protestant advocates, before the bar of enlightened public opinion, for judgment in
the case. Roman Catholics misrepresent their own creed, their Church,
and its corrupt institutions. The most revolting, wicked, and immoral
features of their *holy and immutable system,* are kept out of sight by
its corrupt Clergy, and Jesuitical teachers; while, with a purpose to
deceive, a *Protestant sense* is attached to most of their doctrines and
peculiarities. By this vile means, they designedly *misrepresent themselves,* and impose on the public, by inducing charitable and unin-
formed persons to believe that they are not as profligate as they are
represented to be. . . . One of the most alarming "signs of the times"
is, that while Protestant ministers, of different persuasions, only two
brief years ago, could preach with power and eloquence against the

William G. Brownlow, *Americanism Contrasted with Foreignism, Romanism, and Bogus Democracy* (Nashville, 1856), pp. 4-8, 36, 54-55, 58-60,
106.

dogmas and corrupting tendencies of *Romanism,* and pass out of the doors of their churches, receiving the compliments and extravagant praises of their entire congregations, let one of them now dare to hold up this Corporation as a dangerous foreign enemy—let him warn his charge against the influence of Popery, or but only designate the Catholic Hierarchy as the "man of sin" described in the Scriptures, and one half of his congregation are grossly insulted: they charge him with meddling in politics; and, by way of resentment, they will either not hear him again, or they will starve him out, by refusing to contribute to his support . . . !

Popery is a system of mere human policy; altogether of Foreign origin; Foreign in its support; importing Foreign vassals and paupers by multiplied thousands; and sending into every State and Territory in this Union, a most baneful Foreign and anti-Republican influence. Its old *goutified,* immoral, and drunken Pope, his Bishops and Priests, are *politicians;* men of the world, earthly, sensual, and devilish, and mere men of pleasure. Associated with them for the purpose, in great State and National contests, of securing the Catholic vote, are the worst class of American politicians, designing demagogues, selfish office-seekers, and bad men, calling themselves *Democrats* and "Old-Line Whigs!" These politicians know that Popery, as a system, is in the hands of a Foreign despotism, precisely what the Koran is in the hands of the Grand Turk and his partisans. But corrupt and ambitious politicians in this country, are willing to act the part of traitors to our laws and Constitution, for the sake of profitable offices; and they are willing to sacrifice the Protestant Religion, on the ancient and profligate altar at Rome, if they may but rise to distinction on its ruins!

The great Democratic party of this country, which has degenerated into a *Semi-Papal Organization,* for the base purposes of power and plunder, now fully partakes of the intolerant spirit of Rome, and is acting it out in all the departments of our State and General Governments. What Romanism has been to the Old World, this Papal and Anti-American organization seeks and promises to be to this country. What is Popery in Roman Catholic Europe? It is as intolerant in politics as in religion: it taxes and oppresses the subjects and citizens of every country; it interdicts nations; dethrones governors, chief magistrates, and kings; dissolves civil governments; suspends commerce; annuls civil laws; and, to gratify its unsanctified lust of ambition, it has overrun whole nations with bloodshed, and thrown them into confusion. So it is with this *"Bogus"* Democracy: it wages a war of extermination against the freedom of the press, and against the liberty of speech, the rights of human conscience, and the liberties of man: hence its indiscriminate proscription of all who dare to unite with the AMERICAN PARTY, or openly espouse their cause. Popery aims at universal power over the bodies and souls of all men; and history proclaims that its weapons have been dungeons, racks, chains, fire, and sword! The *bastard* Democracy of the present age has united with the Prelates, Priests, Monks, and Nuns of Romanism, and is daily affiliating with hundreds of thousands of the very off-scourings of the European Catholic population—stimulating them to deeds of violence, and to the shedding of blood . . . !

Under the guidance of an ALL-WISE PROVIDENCE, the Protector of our Republic, and of the Protestant Religion, it is in the power of the free and independent voters of these United States to cause this enemy's long *"arm to be clean dried up, and* his *right eye to be utterly darkened,"* by elevating to the two first offices within the gift of the world, MILLARD FILLMORE and ANDREW J. DONELSON!

I believe the hand of God to be in this very movement. . . . I regard the movement as one growing out of a great crisis in the affairs of our country, and a precursor of a sound, healthful, and vigorous nationality, and which will ultimately prevent the liberties of this country from being destroyed, by the machinations of such demagogues and factionists as now seek to *excuse* Romanism, and fellowship Foreign Pauperism. . . .

Every Roman Catholic in the known world is under the absolute control of the Catholic Priesthood, by considerations not only of a temporal, but an eternal weight. This is what gives their Priesthood such power and influence in elections; an influence they are using in every State, against the American party. And it is this faculty of concentration, this political influence, this power of the Priesthood to control the Catholic community, and cause a vast multitude of ignorant foreigners to vote as a *unit,* and thus control the will of the American people, that has engendered this opposition to the Catholic Church. It is this aggressive policy and corrupting tendency of the Romish Church; this organized and concentrated political power of a distinct class of men; foreign by birth; inferior in intelligence and virtue to the American people, and not their religion and form of worship, objectionable as these are known to be, which have called forth the opposition of the American party to the Catholic Church. . . .

It is a matter of utter astonishment to find a great political party in this country, most of whom are native-born Protestants, taking sides with a foreign Church, whose designs against this country . . . are of the most wicked and fearful character. . . . In the wild hunt for territory by the progressive Democracy, and their efforts to settle our Western lands with foreigners who are to a man Free Soilers and Abolitionists, the South has more to fear than from all other considerations. What is Gov. Johnson's iniquitous Homestead bill, but a bid for foreigners? He proposes to give to the heads of families one hundred and sixty acres of land, thus *hiring* all the convicts and paupers of Europe to come and settle in our Western States and Territories! Sir, but let your progressive, sublimated, double-distilled, converging-lines, Johnsonian Democracy bring into this Union one million of Spanish Papists—black, brown, sorrel, and tawny—under the guise of acquiring Cuba for the South: let them bring eight hundred thousand French and English Papists, under the name of acquiring Canada for the North: let them bring two millions of Mexican Papists—brown, tawny, red and black, being a mixture of all colors and all nations—under the specious pretence of "extending the area of freedom"—let all this be done—and your party, made up of native traitors, and foreign vagabonds, and Catholic paupers, are aiming at it—let it be done, I say, and farewell to liberty, and all that is sacred in this country! With five millions of Papists in our midst—four millions and a half being of foreign birth, and four millions speaking a foreign language —all taught from infancy to hate and detest Protestantism as a crime —an American party would become an absolute political necessity.

The aim of the American party is, by fair party means, to correct a great social evil and political wrong; and if they cannot do that, to prevent its *further increase.* . . .

From Maine to the shores of the Pacific the country is convulsed with intense excitement upon this subject. Shall Americans govern themselves, or shall Foreigners, unacquainted with our laws, and brought up under monarchical governments rule? Shall those who are temporarily and spiritually subject to a foreign prince be our legislators, postmasters, foreign ministers, and military leaders, and change our laws as they are directed by the Pope of Rome? Such results the

American party have set out to prevent. The present excitement will not cease; true Americans and Protestants will labor and pray until our distracted country shall be redeemed from the influence of civil and ecclesiastical tyranny. . . .

The Romish Hierarchy is far more numerous in *Protestant* America than in any Catholic country on earth. Their strength in America equals what it is in Ireland, Scotland and England combined! How extensive is this religious organization in our land: how subtle! Its ramifications are all so many *arteries* which receive their life's blood from the heart at Rome and return it there by its regular palpitations! It is now concentrating its *arteries* at Washington city, and is promised "aid and comfort" from the great Democratic party—a party fast becoming the foe of true liberty, and of the evangelical Protestant faith.

source 6

More Destructive to Human Life Than War, Famine, Pestilence, and Fire . . .

Rufus W. Clark

It is my purpose in this little manual, to present, in a direct and concise form, the prominent arguments in favor of the Massachusetts Anti-Liquor Law. . . . There is not a moral or political question within the range of legislative authority, in which the rich and the poor, and those of every age and rank in society, are so deeply interested as in this. It is, more than any other, vitally connected with the public health and morals, with the security of property and human life, and with the progress of humanity and religion.

Rufus W. Clark, *Fifty Arguments in Favor of Sustaining and Enforcing the Massachusetts Anti-Liquor Law* (Boston, 1853), pp. 3-4, 15-16, 18-19, 32, 35, 44-46.

All intelligent, wise, and good men unite in the opinion that the traffic in ardent spirits is the cause of more than three fourths of the pauperism, crime, and wretchedness with which society is afflicted; that it is more destructive to human life than war, famine, pestilence, and fire combined; that it sends its miserable victims to the grave in far greater numbers than the legions of Cæsar ever fell upon the battle field, or the armies of Napoleon were ever sacrificed to his cruel ambition. We are ready to prove, that this traffic violates every dictate of humanity, every principle in morals, every law in the decalogue, every obligation that an enlightened man is under to promote the welfare of his fellow-men and the honor of God; that it impedes the progress of civilization, weakens the force of Christianity, and renders abortive many other reforms. We are ready to prove that the monster vice which this traffic sustains fills our almshouses with paupers, our jails with criminals, our asylums with maniacs, and makes the drunkard's home a hell; that it arms the insane murderer with deadly weapons, and lets loose the fiend upon society; that it sends forth the midnight incendiary upon his fearful mission; palsies the mariner upon the ocean, and leaves the richly-freighted ship to be dashed upon the rocks, and the crew to sink in the dark waters. On sea and land, in city, town, and village, upon the mountains, in the valleys and plains, its ravages are discernible.

Such is the evil which the Massachusetts legislature, prompted by a sense of humanity and justice, has undertaken to suppress by the force of law. Between this infernal traffic and society it has placed this Anti-Liquor Law, that it may crush the former and protect the latter; that it may stay the desolating torrent, and save the young and future generations from being swallowed up in the fearful vortex. Shall this law be sustained and enforced? On the affirmative of this question I submit fifty arguments, drawn from the most authentic sources, and entitled to the serious consideration of every thinking, humane, and Christian man.

PAUPERISM

According to the Report for 1850, there were in this state fourteen thousand six hundred and seventy four paupers, made such, directly or indirectly, by intemperance. A careful writer says, "Of three thousand persons admitted to the workhouse in Salem, Mass., two thousand nine hundred were brought there directly or indirectly by intemperance. . . ."

In the Annual Report of the "Boston Society for the Prevention of Pauperism" for 1852, I find this statement: "These places (dram shops) are the nurseries of pauperism, crime and disease, and do more to fill our charitable and criminal institutions, and to swell the bills of mortality, than all other causes put together. All efforts to eradicate pauperism and crime must, in a measure, prove fruitless until these places are closed." . . . Such facts need no comment. . . .

INTEMPERANCE IS THE CHIEF CAUSE OF CRIME

From statistical reports it can be proved that more than four fifths of the crimes which are committed are produced by alcoholic drinks. . . . In many of the prisons scarcely a single inmate can be found who has entirely abstained from intoxicating drinks. . . .

MURDERS COMMITTED

It is estimated that in the United States about one murder is caused every day by the agency of rum; and during the past year, two hundred suicides have, under the influence of intemperance, rushed into the presence of the supreme Judge of the universe. Those engaged in the trials of capital offences testify that of forty-four murders, forty-three were committed by intemperate men, or upon those addicted to this vice. Such a fact seems astounding; and yet, when we consider how intemperance deadens the moral faculties, blasts the conscience, and inflames the worst passions of the soul, turning a human being into a bloodthirsty fiend, we are not astonished at the result. But we are astonished that civilized men will continue to sell an article which they know will lead directly to such fearful consequences. We are amazed that the people who are so vigilant in regard to protecting life from danger from other sources; who insist upon having a railroad accident investigated with the greatest care, that it may be publicly known upon whom the blame rests; who are so ready to shun an apothecary's shop where a single mistake in putting up medicine has been made; who censure and punish a physician for one case of malpractice,—should at the same time sustain a traffic that it is known beforehand will lead to murder and every other crime.

INSANITY

At this hour there are in the state of Massachusetts over three hundred maniacs, whose reason has been dethroned by this accursed evil. Among this number there are young men, who early gave promise of great distinction and usefulness—before whom life opened joyfully and brilliantly, but who, falling into the embrace of the demon Alcohol, had their hopes blasted and their fine intellects shattered. Even the learned professions have contributed their proportion to this unfortunate company. From careful observation, for a series of years, in this country and Great Britain, it was found that, in many parts of both nations, more than fifty per cent. of the insanity was caused by intoxicating drinks. . . .

IDIOCY

From the first state report upon idiocy in Massachusetts, it appears that of fourteen hundred idiots, five hundred were born so in consequence of having drunken parents. . . . With what monuments of the divine displeasure towards this awful sin does the drunken father surround himself! To gaze year after year upon a little group of idiotic children made such by his own vice, to be conscious that he has himself defrauded them of reason, of hope, of happiness, must, if he has any of the feelings of a father, produce the most intense agony.

Emigrants and Intemperance

American Protestant Magazine

It is a significant fact, which deserves the serious attention of the religious public, and of the friends of Temperance particularly, that nine-tenths of the dram shops in the city of New York are kept by foreigners. The relapse into the drinking habits, from which the efforts of temperance men had once so far brought the community at large, which at present strikes the eye of the observer, is traceable more to the influence of these dram-selling shops than to any other cause. . . .

Of late years these shops have been astonishingly on the increase. They have been multiplied till now they greet the passer-by at almost every street-corner of the city. And nearly all of them are kept by foreigners. The number of native American rumsellers is significantly small. Irish and German grocers supply, to a large extent, the growing demand for intoxicating drinks; and the increase of these shops, which is going on at a rate which threatens the morals and health of the city, should excite alarm and compassion in every philanthropic mind.

Now, while the right to sell liquor is as readily to be allowed to a foreigner as a native; and while the *legal* right of any man to do so is not questioned, the fact that intemperance is deriving strength and volume and fearfulness from the character of the emigrants that are pouring in upon us, ought to rouse attention. Something ought to be done to arrest this great and growing evil. Some influence ought to be brought to bear upon this class of men which shall make them see and realize the evil nature of their pursuits. Most of them are doing it ignorantly. They come from countries and from circles where the subject of temperance has received little or no attention—where the

The American Protestant Magazine, IV (February, 1849), pp. 271-73.

idea of wrong has never been associated with the traffic in, or the drinking of ardent spirits. It argues no extraordinary depravity or hard heartedness in the emigrant, fresh from Ireland or Germany, that he pursues what to him seems an honest calling. He is far less culpable in doing it than an American would be. But still the evil is wrought. The flood-gates of intemperance, pauperism and crime are thrown open by them; and if nothing be done to close them, they will carry us back to all the drunkenness and evil of former times. . . .

source 8

Americans Must Rule America

Know-Nothing Platform

III. *Americans must rule America;* and to this end, *native*-born citizens should be selected for all state, federal, or municipal offices of government employment, in preference to naturalized citizens. . . .

V. No person should be selected for political station (whether of native or foreign birth), who recognizes any alliance or obligation of any description to any foreign prince, potentate or power, who refuses to recognize the federal and state constitutions (each within its own sphere), as paramount to all other laws, as rules of particular [political] action.

VIII. An enforcement of the principles that no state or territory can admit other than native-born citizens to the right of suffrage, or of holding political office unless such persons shall have been naturalized according to the laws of the United States.

IX. A change in the laws of naturalization, making a continued residence of twenty-one years, of all not heretofore provided for, an

The Know-Nothing Platform, 1856, reprinted in Kirk H. Porter and Donald Bruce Johnson, *National Party Platforms, 1840-1960* (Urbana, 1961), pp. 22-23. Reprinted by permission.

indispensable requisite for citizenship hereafter, and excluding all paupers or persons convicted of crime from landing upon our shores; but no interference with the vested rights of foreigners.

X. Opposition to any union between Church and State; no interference with religious faith or worship, and no test oaths for office, except those indicated in the 5th section of this platform.

XIII. Opposition to the reckless and unwise policy of the present administration in the general management of our national affairs, and more especially as shown in removing "Americans" (by designation) and conservatives in principle, from office, and placing foreigners and ultraists in their places, . . . as shown in granting to unnaturalized foreigners the right of suffrage in Kansas and Nebraska. . . .

source **9**

Most of Its Members
Were Also Temperance Men

Neal Dow

The prohibitory movement received invaluable assistance from the distinctively anti-slavery element in the state. . . . Most of its members were also temperance men, holding the movement for Prohibition as second only in importance to the object they cherished as above all others. On the other hand, many of us who gave temperance the first position were almost as earnest Free Soilers. . . .

When the Maine Law was adopted, the *Inquirer* . . . the organ of the Free Soilers, was the only paper other than an avowedly temperance publication that gave it a cordial and hearty welcome. Elsewhere it will be shown how in another exigency of Prohibition, the Free Soilers rallied to its defense, and that the two elements became fused into a new political party, pledged to both issues. . . .

The Reminiscences of Neal Dow (Portland, Maine, 1898), pp. 306-7, 495, 502-3, 506-7, 509, 511-12, 514, 518-19.

Whig and Democratic politicians had by this time learned that a larger number of voters than ever were interested in other issues than as to which of their leaders should be placed in office, and were determined that they would be led by none whom they did not believe to be sound upon the great questions of the prohibition of the liquor-traffic and the non-extension of slavery, which they had come to regard as of transcending political importance. How to utilize to the best advantage or to avoid the unfavorable effect of this changed condition . . . were . . . of grave concern to those who sought to evolve from the political chaos of the day the promotion of Prohibition and Free-Soil principles.

Earnestly anti-slavery in my convictions, and irrevocably opposed to the extension of the peculiar institution, I was naturally anxious that Maine should take a right position on that question. But I was determined, so far as I could influence events, that this should be done without imperiling Prohibition. I believed that policy right and its enforcement sure to contribute to the moral weal and the material prosperity of the state, and therefore, a matter of great importance, none more so, to our people. . . .

With a number of other men more or less interested in public affairs, and each, perhaps, actuated by somewhat different motives, I earnestly and industriously addressed myself to bringing about a union at the polls of the various elements which for one reason or another were antagonistic to the old Democratic party in the state.

Before the adjournment of the legislature, in the spring of 1854, signs of political chaos were abundant. The Morrill-Pillsbury breach in the Democratic party had become wider than ever.

The Morrill-Democrats again presented their leader on a platform endorsing the Maine Law and condemning the repeal of the Missouri Compromise. . . . By this time the Whig party had held its state convention, and had adopted a platform similar in its reference to the important issues of Prohibition and slavery to that of the Morrill men. . . .

A state temperance convention was now held, over which I presided. The convention endorsed the candidacy of Mr. Morrill with an unequivocal—as it may easily be believed, for I had drawn it myself—Maine Law resolution, one which, by the way, I had taken the precaution to learn, would be entirely satisfactory to the candidate nominated upon it. This was immediately followed by the Free-Soil endorsement of Mr. Morrill, who was as reliable an exponent of the views of that party upon the slavery issue as he was of the temperance men upon Prohibition. . . .

About this time the Know-Nothing organization had established numerous lodges in the state and had acquired some political strength. . . . The opposition to the Democracy was in the saddle of the order, and just prior to the election its endorsement of Mr. Morrill was secured, much to the disgust of its Democratic contingent. . . .

Before the adjournment of the legislature, the coalition members of both branches united in a call inviting the people of the state, without distinction of former political party, in favor of a prohibitory law and opposed to the further extension of slavery and the encroachment of the slave power, to assemble in a convention to transact the necessary business and organize the Republican party. . . .

The convention was held on the 22nd of February, 1855. . . . Among others, it adopted the following resolution:

> *Resolved,* That the existence and execution of the Maine Temperance Law is a vital element in the organization and life of the Republican party in this state, and is one of the chief safeguards of the lives, reputation, property and homes of our people.

. . . Enough has been said to show that whatever other purposes were contemplated in the organization of the Republican party of Maine, and whatever other agencies served to make way for its accession to power in the state, it may be claimed, without ignoring any of those, that the Maine Law movement was a most important and potential influence to that end.

Platform of the Indiana Republican Party, 1856

The people of Indiana, consisting of all who are opposed to the policy of the present Federal administration . . . now submit to the people the following platform of principles:

Fourth—That we are in favor of the naturalization laws of Congress, with five years probation, and that the right of suffrage should accompany and not precede naturalization.

Fifth—That we believe the General Assembly of the State has the power to prohibit the sale of intoxicating liquors as a beverage, and that we are in favor of a constitutional law which will effectually suppress the evils of intemperance.

Russel M. Seeds, ed., *The History of the Republican Party of Indiana* (Indianapolis, Ind., 1899), p. 25.

To Maintain Inviolate the Rights and Privileges of Adopted Citizens

Thomas Barr

The Democratic party, in all its platforms, has pledged itself to the nation and to the oppressed and downtrodden of the earth to maintain inviolate the rights and privileges of adopted citizens, and frown down any attempt, from any quarter, "to obstruct the laws of naturalization of foreigners. . . ." The narrow, illiberal, bigoted policy which proscribes citizens because of their religious belief, or the accident of birthplace, dating its commencement from the vice presidential term of John Adams, and culminating in the alien and sedition laws . . . has ever met with the most determined opposition of the national Democratic party. . . . Whatever may be the result of the coming conventions at Baltimore and Richmond . . . place your trust and lend your best energies to the principles and men having the broad endorsement of the national Democracy. While it triumphs, your liberties and your rights are sacred and safe. Let it be vanquished, and if they allow you to live at all, it will be as "hewers of wood and drawers of water." I speak to you, my fellow-Catholic and foreign-born citizens, honestly and truly, because your wrongs are my wrongs, your triumph is my triumph also.

Had the Republican party nominated WILLIAM H. SEWARD as their candidate for the highest office in the gift of the people, I might, perhaps, have modified . . . the terms by which I have characterized the hostility of that party to Catholic and foreign-born citizens, because that distinguished statesman has ever borne himself, in his public and private character, with liberality, kindness, and generosity towards both these classes of our fellow-citizens. And, perhaps, in this honorable trait of his political character may be found one, if not the chief

Representative Thomas Barr (D-New York), June 16, 1860, *Congressional Globe*, 36th Cong., 1st sess., pp. 444-45.

cause of his indecent shelving at Chicago by the representatives of a party which owes to him all its claims to national strength at the present day. He had too often and too honestly spoken out his sentiments in favor of the constitutional rights of Catholics and foreign-born citizens, both in State and Federal relations, to give a hope to the Chicago managers of securing the aid of the Know Nothing Americans. Hence, we can explain the vile falsehoods uttered against the Catholic religion . . . told recently in the Senate Chamber by the calumniator of States and men, and, meaner still, the reviler of holy women, the abolition monomaniac of Massachusetts. But as he is the senatorial mouthpiece of the Chicago nominee, I allude to him only to show to my Catholic and foreign-born fellow-citizens that there is no difference, as respects their rights and privileges, between the disguised Know-Nothingism of Chicago and the avowed Americanism of Baltimore. They are the Scylla and Charybdis between which, if we wish to enjoy the constitutional privileges for which our fathers shed their blood, we must endeavor to pass. To do so in safety, we must cling to the fortunes of the good old Democratic ship, which alone can brave the storm and avoid the dangers of whirlpool and shoal, with the stars and stripes at its masthead and the Constitution its chart.

To Degrade the Foreign White Man

California State Democratic Party

Resolved, That the Republican Party of the State of Massachusetts have, by incorporating in their Constitution a provision requiring of the naturalized citizen a residence of two years after naturalization, in order to enjoy the right of suffrage or the privilege of holding office, and yet at the same time allowing those privileges even to the fugitive slave upon a residence of one year, attempted to degrade the foreign white man below the level of the negro and the mulatto, and that we, the Democracy of California, utterly repudiate such infamous doctrine.

Resolution of the California State Democratic Party, 1859. Copy in Jefferson Davis Papers, Library of Congress, June 1859 folder.

Upon This Subject the North Has Yielded Until There Is No More to Give Up

David Wilmot

What . . . do we ask? That free territory shall remain free. We demand the neutrality of this Government upon the question of slavery. Is there any complexion of Abolitionism in this, sir? I have stood up at home, and battled, time and again, against the Abolitionists of the North. I have assailed them publicly, upon all occasions, when it was proper to do so. I have met them in their own meetings, and face to face combatted them. Any efforts, sir, that may be made, here or elsewhere, to give an Abolition character to this movement, cannot, so far as my district and my people are concerned, have the least effect. Any efforts made to give to me the character of an Abolitionist will fall harmless. . . . I stand ready at all times, and upon all occasions, as do nearly the entire North, to sustain the institutions of the South as they exist. When the day of trial comes, as many, many southern men fear it may come, we stand ready, with our money and our blood, to rush to the rescue. When that day comes, sir, the North will stand, shoulder to shoulder with their brethren of the South. We stand by the Constitution and all its compromises.

But, sir, the issue now presented is not whether slavery shall exist unmolested where it now is, but whether it shall be carried to new and distant regions, now free, where the footprint of a slave cannot be found. This, sir, is the issue. Upon it I take my stand, and from it I cannot be frightened or driven by idle charges of abolitionism. I ask not that slavery be abolished. I demand that this Government preserve the integrity of *free territory* against the aggressions of slavery—

David Wilmot, February 8, 1847, *Congressional Globe,* 29th Cong., 2d sess., *Appendix,* pp. 315-18.

against its wrongful usurpations. . . . We are told, that the joint blood and treasure of the whole country being expended in this acquisition, therefore it should be divided, and slavery allowed to take its share. Sir, the South has her share already; the installment for slavery was paid in advance. We are fighting this war for Texas and for the South. I affirm it—every intelligent man knows it—Texas is the primary cause of this war. For this, sir, northern treasure is being exhausted, and northern blood poured out upon the plains of Mexico. We are fighting this war cheerfully, not reluctantly—cheerfully fighting this war for Texas; and yet we seek not to change the character of her institutions. Slavery is there: there let it remain. Sir, the whole history of this question is a history of concessions on the part of the North. . . . Three slave States have been admitted out of the Louisiana purchase. The slave State of Florida has been received into the Union; and Texas annexed, with the privilege of making five States out of her territory. What has the North obtained from these vast acquisitions, purchased by the joint treasure and defended by the common blood of the Union? One State, sir—one: young Iowa, just admitted into the Union, and not yet represented on the floor of the Senate. This, sir, is a history of our acquisitions since we became a nation. A history of northern concession—of southern triumphs. . . . There is no question of abolition here, sir. Shall the South be permitted, by aggression, by invasion of the right, by subduing free territory, and planting slavery upon it, to wrest these provinces from northern freemen, and turn them to the accomplishment of their own sectional purposes and schemes? This is the question. Men of the North answer. Shall it be so? Shall we of the North submit to it? If we do, we are coward slaves, and deserve to have the manacles fastened upon our own limbs. . . .

When, sir, in God's name, will the time come for the North to speak out? Our standard is in California—our flag floats over New Mexico. The organ of the Administration proclaims to the world that these territories are ours, not to be *"abandoned, sacrificed, or surrendered:"* our troops are there, and an armed body of emigrants has been sent forward permanently to occupy and hold the country. The whole South rise up here, and declare that they will plant slavery in those countries; and yet we are told that it is not time for the North to act; this, too, by northern men! One finds an excuse for the betrayal of the North, under the declaration that he "believes no territory will be acquired;" another denounces my amendment as "puerile, out of time and out of place;" a third seeks refuge from the indignation of a betrayed constituency, under the idle plea that my proposition embarrasses the Administration, and tends to prevent a vigorous prosecution of the war. . . .

The South is true to her supposed interest on this question. Once, sir, the North, too, stood true on this question. The State of Penn was true to her character and her history. Every Representative from Pennsylvania who was present voted at the last session in favor of the proviso I offered. I trust it will be so again. We shall see. Why, sir, should we fear for the action of northern men on this question? It is right, sir; it is just; it is timely. If ever a declaration against the extension of slavery over a free territory is to be effectual, it must be made now. Wait! Why, sir, while we are waiting slavery is pushing onward. Already has the southern slavery of this Union been transplanted into New Mexico. The fundamental law which General Kearny laid down for the government of that country bears the impress and proves the existence of slavery. Yes, sir, slavery is there, yet northern men advise delay: sneer, sir, at this movement as "puerile and childish. . . ."

Already, sir, on the route of travel between Missouri and New Mexico slaves are found, who are being removed thither. Slavery is there, sir—there, in defiance of law. Slavery does not wait for all the forms of annexation to be consummated. It is on the move, sir. It is in New Mexico. It is in Oregon. Yes, sir, it is in Oregon; and this day, in that distant territory of the Union, does the lash of the Missouri master drive his negro slaves to the field of labor. . . . Yet sir, in the face of all this we are told that our action is premature, untimely. "Wait," says my colleague [Mr. McClean], "until we get the skin of the lion, before we dispute about his hide." Sir, we have the skin, and slavery is already grappling for it. I invoke my colleague to the rescue. I repeat it, sir, now is the time, and the only time. Southern men declare that they desire this question settled now. Neither party should be deceived. The North ought not to be betrayed under the idea held out that slavery cannot, or will not, exist there. Let not the South be deceived. Let no prospect be held out to her that this war is to result in strengthening and extending this institution. Now is the time, and the honest time, to meet this question. . . .

Sir, upon this subject, the North has yielded until there is no more to give up. We have gone on, making one acquisition after another, until we have acquired and brought into the Union every inch of slave territory that was to be found upon this Continent. Now, sir, we have passed beyond the boundaries of slavery and reached free soil. Who is willing to surrender it? Men of the North—Representatives of northern freemen, will you consummate such a deed of infamy and shame? I trust in God not. Oh! for the honor of the North—for the fair fame of our green hills and valleys, be firm in this crisis—be true to your country and your race. The white laborer of the North claims your service; he demands that you stand firm to his interests and his rights; that you preserve the future homes of his children, on the distant shores of the Pacific, from the degradation and dishonor of negro servitude. Where the negro slave labors, the free white man cannot labor by his side without sharing in his degradation and disgrace. . . .

Sir, as a friend of the Union, as a lover of my country, and in no spirit of hostility to the South, I offered my amendment. Viewing slavery as I do, I must resist its further extension and propagation on the North American continent. It is an evil, the magnitude of which, no man can see.

source **14**

For the Sake of Freedom

Free-Soil Platform

Whereas, We have assembled in Convention, as a union of *Freemen,* for the sake of Freedom, forgetting all past political differences in a common resolve to maintain the rights of Free Labor against the aggressions of the Slave Power, and to secure Free Soil for a Free People:

The Free-Soil Platform, 1848, in Porter and Johnson, *op. cit.,* pp. 13-14. Reprinted by permission.

And whereas, The political Conventions recently assembled at Baltimore and Philadelphia, have dissolved the national party organizations heretofore existing, by nominating for the Chief Magistracy of the United States, under Slaveholding dictation, candidates, *neither of whom* can be supported by the opponents of Slavery-extension, without a *sacrifice of consistency, duty,* and *self-respect.*

And whereas, These nominations, so made, furnish the occasion and demonstrate the necessity of the union of the People under the banners of Free Democracy, in a solemn and formal *declaration* of their *independence* of the *Slave Power,* and of their fixed determination to rescue the Federal Government from its control:

Resolved, therefore . . . ,

That Slavery in the several States of this Union which recognize its existence, depends upon the State laws alone, which cannot be repealed or modified by the Federal Government, and for which laws that Government is not responsible. We therefore propose no interference by Congress with Slavery within the limits of any State.

Resolved, That the PROVISO of Jefferson, to prohibit the existence of Slavery, after 1800 in all the Territories of the United States, Southern and Northern; the votes of six States, and sixteen delegates, in the Congress of 1784, for the Proviso, to three States and seven delegates against it; the actual exclusion of Slavery from the Northwestern Territory by the ORDINANCE OF 1787, *unanimously* adopted by the States in Congress, and the entire history of that period, clearly show that it was the settled policy of the nation, *not to extend, nationalize,* or *encourage,* but to limit, localize, and discourage, Slavery; and to *this policy* which should never have been departed from, the Government ought to *return.*

Resolved, That in the judgment of this Convention, Congress has no more power to make a SLAVE than to make a KING; no more power to institute or establish SLAVERY, than to institute or establish a MONARCHY. No such power can be found among those specifically conferred by the Constitution, or derived by just implication from them.

Resolved, THAT IT IS THE DUTY OF THE FEDERAL GOVERNMENT TO RELIEVE ITSELF FROM ALL RESPONSIBILITY FOR THE EXISTENCE OR CONTINUANCE OF SLAVERY WHEREVER THAT GOVERNMENT POSSESS CONSTITUTIONAL POWER TO LEGISLATE ON THAT SUBJECT, AND IS THUS RESPONSIBLE FOR ITS EXISTENCE.

Resolved, That the true, and, in the judgment of this Convention, the *only* safe means of preventing the extension of Slavery into territory now free, is to prohibit its existence in all such territory by *an act of Congress.*

Resolved, That we accept the issue which the Slave Power has forced upon us, and to their demand for more Slave States and more Slave Territory, our calm but final answer is: No more Slave States and no more Slave Territory. Let the soil of our extensive domains be kept free, for the hardy pioneers of our own land, and the oppressed and banished of other lands seeking homes of comfort and fields of enterprise in the New World. . . .

source 15

Finality Plank of the Democracy, 1852

Democratic Party Platform

. . . The democratic party of the Union, standing on this national platform, will abide by and adhere to a faithful execution of the acts known as the compromise measures settled by the last Congress. . . .
. . . The democratic party will resist all attempts at renewing, in Congress or out of it, the agitation of the slavery question, under whatever shape or color the attempt may be made.

Porter and Johnson, *op. cit.,* p. 17. Reprinted by permission

source 16

It Is Slavery That Renews the Strife

Salmon P. Chase

A few of us . . . never believed that the acts of 1850 would prove to be a permanent adjustment of the slavery question. We believed no permanent adjustment of that question possible except by a return to the original policy of the fathers of the Republic, by which slavery was restricted within State limits, and freedom, without exception or limitation, was intended to be secured to every person outside of State limits and under the exclusive jurisdiction of the General Government.

But, sir, we only represented a small, though vigorous and growing, party in the country. Our number was small in Congress. By some we were regarded as visionaries—by some as factionists; while almost all agreed in pronouncing us mistaken.

And so, sir, the country was at peace. As the eye swept the entire circumference of the horizon and upward to mid-heaven not a cloud appeared; to common observation there was no mist or stain upon the clearness of the sky.

But suddenly all is changed. Rattling thunder breaks from the cloudless firmament. The storm bursts forth in fury. Warring winds rush into conflict. . . . And now we find ourselves in the midst of an agitation, the end and issue of which no man can foresee.

Now, sir, who is responsible for this renewal of strife and controversy? Not we, for we have introduced no question of territorial slavery into Congress—not we who are denounced as agitators and factionists. No, sir: the quietists and the finalists have become agitators; they who told us that all agitation was quieted, and that the reso-

Senator Salmon P. Chase, February 3, 1854, *Congressional Globe*, 33rd Cong., 1st sess., *Appendix*, pp. 133-34, 139-40.

lutions of the political conventions put a final period to the discussion of slavery.

This will not escape the observation of the country. It is *Slavery* that renews the strife. It is Slavery that again wants room. It is Slavery, with its insatiate demands for more slave territory and more slave States.

And what does Slavery ask for now? Why, sir, it demands that a time-honored and sacred compact shall be rescinded—a compact which has endured through a whole generation—a compact which has been universally regarded as inviolable, North and South—a compact, the constitutionality of which few have doubted, and by which all have consented to abide. . . .

Mr. President, three great eras have marked the history of this country, in respect to slavery. The first may be characterized as the Era of ENFRANCHISEMENT. It commenced with the earliest struggles for national independence. The spirit which inspired it animated the hearts and prompted the efforts . . . of all the great men of our early history. All these hoped—all these labored for—all these believed in the final deliverance of the country from the curse of slavery. . . . Under its influence . . . State after State provided for the emancipation of the slaves within their limits, prior to the adoption of the Constitution. . . .

This second era was the Era of CONSERVATISM. Its great maxim was to preserve the existing condition. Men said, let things remain as they are; let slavery stay where it is; exclude it where it is not; refrain from disturbing the public quiet by agitation; adjust all differences that arise, not by the application of principles, but by compromises. . . .

The Era of CONSERVATISM passed, also by imperceptible gradations, into the Era of SLAVERY PROPAGANDISM. Under the influences of this new spirit we opened the whole territory acquired from Mexico, except California, to the ingress of slavery. Every foot of it was covered by a Mexican prohibition; and yet, by the legislation of 1850, we consented to expose it to the introduction of slaves. Some, I believe, have actually been carried into Utah and into New Mexico. They may be few, perhaps, but a few are enough to affect materially the probable character of their future governments. Under the evil influences of the same spirit, we are now called upon to reverse the original policy of the Republic; to subvert even a solemn compact of the conservative period, and open Nebraska to slavery.

Sir, I believe that we are upon the verge of another era. That era will be the Era of REACTION. The introduction of this question here, and its discussion, will greatly hasten its advent. We, who insist upon the denationalization of slavery, and upon the absolute divorce of the General Government from all connection with it, will stand with the men who favored the compromise acts, and who yet wish to adhere to them, in their letter and in their spirit, against the repeal of the Missouri prohibition. But you may pass it here. You may send it to the other House. It may become law. But its effect will be to satisfy all thinking men that no compromises with slavery will endure, except so long as they serve the interests of slavery and that there is no safe and honorable ground for non-slaveholders to stand upon, except that of restricting slavery within State limits, and excluding it absolutely from the whole sphere of Federal jurisdiction. The old questions between political parties are at rest. No great question so thoroughly possesses the public mind as this of slavery. This discussion will hasten the inevitable reorganization of parties upon the new issues which our circumstances suggest. It will light up a fire in the country which may, perhaps, consume those who kindle it. . . .

I repeat, sir, that we who maintain these principles will stand shoulder to shoulder with the men who, differing from us upon other questions, will yet unite with us in opposition to the violation of plighted faith contemplated by this bill. There are men, and not a few, who are willing to adhere to the compromises of 1850. If the Missouri prohibition, which those compromises incorporates and preserves among its own provisions, shall be repealed, abrogated, broken up, thousands will say, Away with all compromises; they are not worth the paper on which they are printed; we will return to the old principles of the Constitution. We will assert the ancient doctrine, that no person shall be deprived of life, liberty, or property, by the legislation of Congress, without due process of law. Carrying out that principle into its practical applications, we will not cease our efforts until slavery shall cease to exist wherever it can be reached by the constitutional action of the Government.

The Crime Against Kansas

Charles Sumner

Mr. President, you are now called to redress a great transgression. Seldom in the history of nations has such a question been presented. Tariffs, Army bills, Navy bills, Land bills, are important, and justly occupy your care; but these all belong to the course of ordinary legislation. As means and instruments only, they are necessarily subordinate to the conservation of Government itself. Grant them or deny them, in greater or less degree, and you will inflict no shock. The machinery of Government will continue to move. The State will not cease to exist. Far otherwise is it with the eminent question now before you, involving, as it does, Liberty in a broad Territory, and also involving the peace of the whole country with our good name in history forever more. . . .

Against this Territory, thus fortunate in position and population, a Crime has been committed, which is without example in the records of the Past. Not in plundered provinces or in the cruelties of selfish governors will you find its parallel. . . .

But the wickedness which I now begin to expose is immeasurably aggravated by the motive which prompted it. Not in any common lust for power did this uncommon tragedy have its origin. It is the rape of a virgin Territory, compelling it to the hateful embrace of Slavery; and it may be clearly traced to a depraved longing for a new slave State, the hideous offspring of such a crime, in the hope of adding to the power of Slavery in the National Government. Yes, sir, when the whole world, alike Christian and Turk, is rising up to condemn this wrong, and to make it a hissing to the nations, here in our Re-

Senator Charles Sumner, May 19, 20, 1856, *Congressional Globe,* 34th Cong., 1st sess., *Appendix,* pp. 529-30, 532, 535, 543-44.

public, *force*—ay, sir, FORCE—has been openly employed in compelling Kansas to this pollution, and all for the sake of political power. There is the simple fact, which you will vainly attempt to deny, but which in itself presents an essential wickedness that makes other public crimes seem like public virtues. . . .

The fury of the propagandists of Slavery, and the calm determination of their opponents, are now diffused from the distant Territory over wide-spread communities, and the whole country, in all its extent—marshaling hostile divisions, and foreshadowing a strife, which, unless happily averted by the triumph of Freedom, will become war —fratricidal, parricidal war—with an accumulated wickedness beyond the wickedness of any war in human annals; justly provoking the avenging judgment of Providence and the avenging pen of history. . . . Now, the Nebraska Bill, on its very face, openly cleared the way for Slavery, and it is not wrong to presume that its originators intended the natural consequences of such an act, and sought in this way to extend Slavery. Of course, they did. And this is the first stage in the Crime against Kansas.

But this was speedily followed by other developments. The barefaced scheme was soon whispered, that Kansas must be a slave State. In conformity with this idea was the Government of this unhappy Territory organized in all its departments; and thus did the President, by whose complicity the Prohibition of Slavery had been overthrown, lend himself to a new complicity—giving to the conspirators a lease of connivance, amounting even to copartnership. The Governor, Secretary, Chief Justice, Associate Justices, Attorney, and Marshal, with a whole caucus of other stipendiaries, nominated by the President and confirmed by the Senate, were all commended as friendly to Slavery. No man, with the sentiments of Washington, or Jefferson, or Franklin, found any favor; nor is it too much to say, that had these great patriots once more come among us, not one of them, with his recorded unretracted opinions on Slavery, could have been nominated by the President or confirmed by the Senate for any post in that Territory. With such auspices the conspiracy proceeded. Even in advance of the Nebraska Bill, secret societies were organized in Missouri, ostensibly to protect her institutions, and afterwards, under the name of "Self-Defensive Associations," and of "Blue Lodges," these were multiplied throughout the western counties of that State, *before any counter-movement from the North*. It was confidently anticipated, that, by the activity of these societies, and the interest of slaveholders everywhere, with the advantage derived from the neighborhood of Missouri, and the influence of the Territorial Government, Slavery might be introduced into Kansas, quietly but surely, without arousing a conflict— that the crocodile egg might be stealthily dropped in the sun-burnt soil, there to be hatched unobserved until it sent forth its reptile monster. . . .

Thus was the Crime consummated. Slavery now stands erect, clanking its chains on the Territory of Kansas, surrounded by a code of death, and trampling upon all cherished liberties, whether of speech, the press, the bar, the trial by jury, or the electoral franchise. And, sir, all this has been done, not merely to introduce a wrong which in itself is a denial of all rights, and in dread of which a mother has lately taken the life of her offspring; not merely, as has been sometimes said, to protect Slavery in Missouri, since it is futile for this State to complain of Freedom on the side of Kansas, when Freedom exists without complaint on the side of Iowa and also on the side of Illinois; but it has been done for the sake of political power, in order to bring two new slaveholding Senators upon this floor, and thus to fortify in the National Government the desperate chances of a waning Oligarchy. . . .

Sir, all this was done in the name of Popular Sovereignty. And this is the close of the tragedy. Popular Sovereignty, which, when truly understood, is a fountain of just power, has ended in Popular Slavery; not merely in the subjection of the unhappy African race, but of this proud Caucasian blood, which you boast. The profession with which you began, of *All by the People*, has been lost in the wretched reality of *Nothing for the People*. Popular Sovereignty, in whose deceitful name plighted faith was broken, and an ancient Landmark of Freedom was overturned, now lifts itself before us, like Sin. . . .

To overthrow this Usurpation is now the special, importunate duty of Congress, admitting of no hesitation or postponement. To this end it must lift itself from the cabals of candidates, the machinations of party, and the low level of vulgar strife. It must turn from that Slave Oligarchy which now controls the Republic, and refuse to be its tool. Let its power be stretched forth towards this distant Territory, not to bind, but to unbind; not for the oppression of the weak, but for the subversion of the tyrannical; not for the prop and maintenance of a revolting Usurpation, but for the confirmation of Liberty. . . .

Let it now take its stand between the living and dead, and cause this plague to be stayed. All this it can do; and if the interests of Slavery did not oppose, all this it would do at once, in reverent regard for justice, law, and order, driving far away all the alarms of war; nor would it dare to brave the shame and punishment of this Great Refusal. But the Slave Power dares anything; and it can be conquered only by the united masses of the People. From Congress to the People, I appeal. . . .

Sir, the people of Kansas, bone of your bone and flesh of your flesh, with the education of freemen and the rights of American citizens, now stand at your door. Will you send them away, or bid them enter? Will you push them back to renew their struggles with a deadly foe, or will you preserve them in security and peace? Will you cast them again into the den of Tyranny, or will you help their despairing efforts to escape? These questions I put with no common solicitude; for I feel that on their just determination depend all the most precious interests of the Republic; and I perceive too clearly the prejudices in the way, and the accumulating bitterness against this distant people, now claiming their simple birthright, while I am bowed with mortification, as I recognize the President of the United States, who should have been a staff to the weak and a shield to the innocent, at the head of this strange oppression.

Barbarous and Cowardly Brutality

New York Tribune

The predominant purpose which should fill the mind of every patriot . . . is to expel from power the party that now controls the government. . . . That party is hopelessly sold to the Nullifiers and Slavery Extensionists. . . . By the indescribable wickedness of men whose ruling passion is the thirst for office, the peace of the country has been wantonly broken, and we are brought to the verge of civil war. . . . A most corrupt party, swaying a weak conscienceless, brain- less President, has disgraced and well nigh ruined the Republic; it is now for the people to rise and restore peace and order. . . .

This is an unexamplified crisis in our history. Never before was the Constitution so tried as now. We have had struggles and agitators, but never before the shocking and alarming spectacle of the Federal Executive using all power to sustain the murder and robbery of inno- cent freemen for the purpose of forcing the institution of Slavery upon a people who abhor it, and are resolved to die rather than submit to such unheard of tyranny and outrage. Never before has a Senator, the representative of a sovereign State, been stricken down in his seat by barbarous and cowardly brutality, for words uttered in debate, and with the Administration, and the party that elected it and has sus- tained it, all standing by tacitly if not openly, to approve and justify the crime. The fundamental rights of the people assailed with civil war in Kansas, and the rights of the States assailed with murderous violence in the Senate—such are the achievements which stamp with odium and with execration the career of this Administration and of this party, marking both for overthrow at the hands of the disgusted and indignant masses.

New York Tribune, June 11, 1856, p. 4.

It is folly to say that this party will pursue a different course. . . .
That party is irredeemably lost. It cannot be made anything else than
a party for the extension of slavery and the subjugation of Freedom.

source **19**

The Sumner Discipline—
The Needful Remedy

Richmond Enquirer

A few Southern journals . . . unite with the abolition papers in
condemning the chastisement inflicted upon Sumner by the Hon. P. S.
Brooks. We have no patience with these mealy-mouthed pharisees of
the Press. . . .

In the main the press of the South applaud the conduct of Mr.
Brooks, without condition or limitation. Our approbation at least is
entire and unreserved. We consider the act good in conception, better
in execution, and best of all in consequence. These vulgar abolitionists
in the Senate are getting above themselves. . . . They are a low,
mean, scurvy set, with some little book learning, but as utterly devoid
of spirit or honor as a pack of curs. . . . The truth is they have been
suffered to run too long without collars. They must be lashed into
submission. Sumner, in particular, ought to have nine and thirty every
morning. . . . Hale is another huge, red face, sweating, scoundrel,
whom some gentlemen should kick and cuff until he abates something
of his impudent talk. . . . [These men] can be brought to reason only
by an application of cowhide or gutta percha. Let them once understand that for every vile word spoken against the South they will
suffer so many stripes, and they will soon learn to behave themselves
like decent dogs—they can never be gentlemen. Mr. Brooks has initi-
ated this salutary discipline, and he deserves applause for the bold,

Richmond Enquirer, June 2, 1856.

judicious manner in which he chastised the scamp Sumner. It was a proper act, done at the proper time, and in the proper place. . . . We trust other gentlemen will follow the example of Mr. Brooks. . . . If need be, let us have a caning or cowhiding every day.

source **20**

When That Party Shall Fail, The Sword Must and Will Do Its Work

Reuben Davis

Mr. Chairman, this is . . . a contest of power against weakness; a contest in which the pride of the freemen of this country is to be humbled and their spirits broken, until they will consent to any degradation, even serfdom; and from this, Mr. Chairman, if our people desire to escape, they must stand by the Democratic organization, and thereby perpetuate the great doctrine of limitation on the powers of the Federal Government, and the absolute right of the States to legislate alone upon subjects which concern their domestic and civil rights —doctrines which leave the people of each State with the full and undivided right to pass for themselves laws suited to their climate, soil, and industrial pursuits.

The perpetuation of the nationality of that party with its principles, leaves every branch of industry free to pursue its own course of policy, and compels it to stand upon its own inherent merits. In its long and brilliant course of triumphs on this continent, it has given no cause of complaint to our people; its career has been unfelt, oppressively. It has discouraged sectionalism and discountenanced class legislation. Against it all class interest have combined and wage war

Reuben Davis, December 22, 1858, *Congressional Globe,* 35th Cong., 2d sess., *Appendix,* p. 69.

of extermination; not because the party had done too much; not because the party had used the power of the Government to advance one interest at the sacrifice of another; but because it had refused to do this—not because it had used the power of the Government to interfere with the domestic interest of the people of the different States, but because it had refused to do it; not because it granted monopolies and gave bounties, but because it had declared that these powers did not belong to the Government; not because it had not vindicated the honor and glory of the nation, when assailed, but because sensitive to national honor it had resented national wrongs; not because it had not used all honorable means to extend our dominion and propagate our free institutions, but because this it had done; not because it had used the power of the Government to prevent the full development of the various sources of wealth and the various branches of industry of our country—our whole country, this it had done, and we see it in the facts that to-day our people are the happiest on earth, the freest on earth, and prosperous beyond all parallel in the past or present history of the world. . . . It is the stern resolve of millions of freemen who know their rights and have resolved to maintain them, who wait for the result of the conflict now being waged in the free States between the constitutional Democracy and those who would trample the Constitution down in a course of usurpation. They await the issue with the most intense interest, but dauntless of the result. This struggle must be ended and sectional strife terminated. As long as the Democratic party is continued in the ascendant, it will be kept in check, and when that party shall fall, the sword must and will do its work.

Platform of the Breckinridge Democrats, 1860

Resolved,

1. That the Government of a Territory organized by an act of Congress is provisional and temporary, and during its existence all citizens of the United States have an equal right to settle with their property in the Territory, without their rights, either of person or property, being destroyed or impaired by Congressional or Territorial legislation.

2. That it is the duty of the Federal Government, in all its departments, to protect, when necessary, the rights of persons and property in the Territories, and wherever else its constitutional authority extends.

3. That when the settlers in a Territory, having an adequate population, form a State Constitution, the right of sovereignty commences, and being consummated by admission into the Union, they stand on an equal footing with the people of other States, and the State thus organized ought to be admitted into the Federal Union, whether its Constitution prohibits or recognizes the institution of slavery.

Porter and Johnson, op. cit., p. 31. Reprinted by permission.

Let Us Go On and Carry Out
Our Destiny. . . .

Andrew Johnson

The first section provides for granting one hundred and sixty acres of land to every head of a family who will emigrate to any of the public domain and settle upon it, and cultivate it for a term of five years. Upon those facts being made known to the register of the land office, he is to be entitled to obtain a patent. The second section provides that he shall make an affidavit, and show to the satisfaction of the officer that his entry is made in good faith, and that his intention is to cultivate the soil and become an actual settler. The sixth section of the bill provides that any person who is now an inhabitant of the United States, but not a citizen, if he makes application, and in the course of five years becomes a citizen of the United States, shall be placed on a footing of equality with the native-born citizens of the country in this respect. The third section provides that those entries shall be confined to land that has been in market, and subjected to private entry; and that the person entering the land shall be confined to each alternate section.

These are substantially the leading provisions of this bill. It does not proceed upon the idea, as some suppose, of making a donation or gift of the public land to the settler. It proceeds upon the principle of consideration, and, as I conceive, and I think many others do, the individual who emigrates to the West, and reclaims and reduces to cultivation one hundred and sixty acres of the public domain, subjecting himself to all the privations and hardships of such a life, pays the highest consideration for his land. . . . If we grant the public lands to actual settlers so as to induce them to settle upon and culti-

Andrew Johnson, May 20, 1858, *Congressional Globe*, 35th Cong., 1st sess., pp. 2265-68, 2272-73.

vate the public lands, can there be anything more national in its character? What is the great object of acquiring territory? Is it not for settlement and cultivation . . . ?

By this bill you provide a man with a home, you increase the revenue, you increase the consumption of home manufactures, and you make him a better man. You give him an interest in the country. His condition is better. There is no man so reliable as he who is interested in the welfare of his country; and who are more interested in the welfare of their country than those who have homes? When a man has a home, he has a deeper, a more abiding interest in the country, and he is more reliable in all things that pertain to the Government. He is more reliable when he goes to the ballot-box; he is more reliable sustaining the stability of our free institutions. . . .

Let us go on and carry out our destiny; interest men in the soil; let your vacant land be divided equally so that men can have homes; let them live by their own industry; and the time will come when this will be the greatest nation on the face of the earth. . . .

Sir, carry out the homestead policy, attach the people to the soil, induce them to love the Government, and you will have the North reconciled to the South, and the South to the North, and we shall not have invidious doctrines preached to stir up bad feelings in either section.

I hope, Mr. President, that this bill will be passed. I think it involves the very first principles of the Government: it is founded upon statesmanship, humanity, philanthropy, and even upon Christianity itself. I know the argument has been made, why permit one portion of the people to go and take some of this land and not another? The law is in general terms; it places it in the power of every man who will go to take a portion of the land.

It was conceded yesterday that the land was owned by the people. There are over three million heads of families in the United States; and if every man who is the head of a family were to take a quarter section of public land, there would still be nearly four million quarter sections left. If some people go and take quarter sections, it does not interfere with the rights of others, for he who goes takes only a part of that which is his, and takes nothing that belongs to anybody else. The domain belongs to the whole people; the equity is in the great mass of the people; the Government holds the fee and passes the title, but the beneficial interest is in the people. There are, as I have

said, two quarter sections of land for every head of a family in the
United States, and we merely propose to permit a head of a family
to take one half of that which belongs to him. . . .

So far as I am concerned—I say it not in any spirit of boast or
egotism—if this bill were passed, and the system it inaugurates carried out, granting a reasonable quantity of land for a man's family,
looking far into the distance to see what is to result from it—a stable,
and industrious, a hardy, a Christian, a philanthropic community
growing out of it, I should feel that the great object of my little mission was fulfilled. All that I desire is the honor and the credit of
being one of the American Congress to consummate and to carry out
this great scheme that is to elevate our race and to make our institutions more permanent. I want no reputation as some have insinuated.
You may talk about Jacobinism, Red Republicanism, and so on. I
pass by such insinuations as the idle wind which I regard not.

I know the motives that prompt me to action. I can go back to
that period in my own history when I could not say I had a home.
This being so, when I cast my eyes from one extreme of the United
States to the other, and behold the great number that are homeless,
I feel for them. I believe this bill would put them in possession of
homes; and I want to see them realizing that sweet conception when
each man can proclaim, "I have a home; an abiding place for my wife
and for my children; I am not the tenant of another; I am my own
ruler; and I will move according to my own will, and not at the dictation of another." Yes, Mr. President, if I should never be heard of
again on the surface of God's habitable globe, the proud and conscious satisfaction of having contributed my little aid to the consum-
mation of this great measure is all the reward I desire.

The people need friends. They have a great deal to bear. They
make all; they do all; but how little they participate in the legislation
of the country? All, or nearly all, of our legislation is for corporations,
for monopolies, for classes, and individuals; but the great mass who
produce all, who make all while we do nothing but consume, are little
cared for; their rights and interests are neglected and overlooked. Let
us, as patriots, let us as statesmen, let us as Christians, consummate
this great measure which will exert an influence throughout the civilized world in fulfilling our destiny.

An Equitable and Just Proportional Legislation

John C. Calhoun

The safe and certain communication between the Gulf of Mexico and the interior States of the West; the improvement and preservation of the navigation of the Mississippi and Ohio Rivers, on which now border ten States and two Territories; the connection of the northern lakes with the Mississippi and Atlantic by a ship canal, and the keeping open the mouths of the Mississippi, so as to be accessible at all times to the largest class of vessels; the fortifying of the gulf and the lake coast, and the erection of additional beacons and light-houses; the increase of our naval marine; the establishment of naval depots, arsenals, dry-docks, armories, founderies, and marine hospitals; the reclaiming a large portion of the public domain now in swamp; the ceding the right of way and alternate sections to railroads passing through the public lands, and the insuring greater certainty and despatch to mail conveyances, whether of steam or magnetic power—are objects not within the jurisdiction of a single State to control, *but common in their benefits to the whole Union,* and within the powers of the General Government. Without, however, speculating on the ceded or reserved rights of the States, your committee feel confident that, under the *commercial jurisdiction* of the General Government, and under the obligations *to provide for the general defence,* and as a *proprietor* of the public domain, there is no power claimed in the resolutions enumerated which may not be legitimately exercised by the Congress of the United States. . . .

The valley of the Mississippi is no longer a Territory or a frontier: it has now become the "bone and sinew"—the centre of the Un-

"The Memphis Memorial," in *The Works of John C. Calhoun,* ed. Richard K. Cralle (New York, 1857), V, 297-99, 301, 309-11.

ion; standing midway between those States on the Atlantic which first gave life and impulse to our free and liberal institutions, and *those* which, under the silent but certain influences of those institutions, are destined to form new stars, to the very borders of the Pacific, in the American constellation. In the rapid progress of improvement, the valley now numbers ten sovereign and independent States, who have become parties to the compact of the old thirteen, and contains ten millions of inhabitants, with an internal and export trade transcending all other parts of like extent and population in the world, and very nearly equal to the entire export and import trade of the United States. Not one tenth of its resources, either in agricultural, commercial, manufacturing, or mineral wealth, has as yet been developed. It is difficult for the most sanguine to estimate or rightly appreciate the destinies yet in store for this favored land of promise. It has, however, but one natural outlet to the highway of nations—but one common channel on which must float to market the annual productive industry of its enterprising and increasing population. This concentration of all its trade—of all its external and internal communications—on but one common avenue, renders it the still more important and necessary that the navigation of that highway for all public purposes should be preserved unimpaired, and its mouths kept unobstructed by the annual alluvial deposits brought down by the descending currents of its tributary streams. Your memorialists are bewildered by the mere speculation of what would be the terrible consequences to the commercial, social, and political relations of these United States, if, like the Nile (an event not at all impossible), the Mississippi should be closed to the *ingress* and *egress* of foreign shipping. That river is as important to States on the Atlantic as is the Atlantic to the communities bordering on the river. They are both highways of commerce, and in all their relations to the States of the Union exercising an influence so *common* in their benefits to the whole, as to demand, as your memorialists believe it will, the supervision and protection of the general representatives in Congress.

    . . . Your memorialists ask no more than an *equitable* and *just proportional* legislation for their *common interests* and *protection* within the legitimate powers of the General Government, which has been and is still annually claiming the consideration and action of your honorable body on the Atlantic and lake sections; they ask, not as a boon, but in *justice* and for common good, that the rivers Mississippi and Ohio be kept open, and their navigation, as far as practicable, be preserved unimpaired at all times to the Gulf. . . .

. . . On the subject of railroads . . . the projects which received the favorable consideration of the convention were roads passing at right angles to the natural outlets or avenues of trade; crossing the ridges and mountains, and intersecting interior districts remote from navigation, and hitherto, from their secluded situation, of little value. They develop, therefor, new sources of agricultural and mineral wealth, and bring into more intimate commercial and political relations the west with the south Atlantic border, hitherto estranged from each other by the interpositions of mountain elevations. . . . Through these roads, in their incipient conception, are made to terminate on the Gulf of Mexico and the Mississippi, they must and will advance with the onward population west, and find no *termini short of the Pacific.*

source 24

The Constitution Has Not . . . Conferred . . . Power to Construct Works of Internal Improvements

James K. Polk

To the House of Representatives:

I have considered a bill entitled "An act making appropriations for the improvement of certain harbors and rivers" . . . and now return the same . . . with my objections to its becoming a law. . . . On examining its provisions and the variety of objects of improvement which it embraces, many of them of a local character, it is difficult to conceive, if it shall be sanctioned and become a law, what practical

President Polk's veto message, August 3, 1846, in *A Compilation of the Messages and Papers of the Presidents,* ed. James Richardson (New York, 1897), pp. 2310-16.

constitutional restraint can hereafter be imposed upon the most extended system of internal improvements by the Federal Government in all parts of the Union. The Constitution has not, in my judgment, conferred upon the Federal Government the power to construct works of internal improvements within the States, or to appropriate money from the Treasury for that purpose. . . . The approved course of the Government and the deliberately expressed judgment of the people have denied the existence of such a power under the Constitution. . . .

A construction of the Constitution so broad as that by which the power in question is defended tends imperceptibly to a consolidation of power in a Government intended by its framers to be thus limited in its authority. "The obvious tendency and inevitable result of a consolidation of the States into one sovereignty would be to transform the republican system of the United States into a monarchy." To guard against the assumption of all powers which encroach upon the reserved sovereignty of the States, and which consequently tend to consolidation, is the duty of all the true friends of our political system. That the power in question is not properly an incident to any of the granted powers I am fully satisfied; but if there were doubts on this subject, experience has demonstrated the wisdom of the rule that all the functionaries of the Federal Government should abstain from the exercise of all questionable or doubtful powers. Some of the objects of appropriation contained in this bill are local in their character, and lie within the limits of a single State; and though in the language of the bill they are called *harbors,* they are not connected with foreign commerce, nor are they places of refuge or shelter for our Navy or commercial marine on the ocean or lake shores. To call the mouth of a creek or a shallow inlet on our coast a harbor can not confer the authority to expend the public money in its improvement. Congress have exercised the power coeval with the Constitution of establishing lighthouses, beacons, buoys, and piers on our ocean and lake shores for the purpose of rendering navigation safe and easy and of affording protection and shelter for our Navy and other shipping. These are safeguards placed in existing channels of navigation. After the long acquiescence of the Government through all preceding Administrations, I am not disposed to question or disturb the authority to make appropriations for such purposes.

When we advance a step beyond this point, and, in addition to the establishment and support, by appropriations from the Treasury, of light-houses, beacons, buoys, piers, and other improvements within the bays, inlets, and harbors on our ocean and lake coasts immediately connected with our foreign commerce, attempt to make improvements in the interior at points unconnected with foreign commerce, and where they are not needed for the protection and security of our Navy and commercial marine, the difficulty arises in drawing a line beyond which appropriations may not be made by the Federal Government. . . .

Should this bill become a law, the same *principle* which authorizes the appropriations which it proposes to make would also authorize similar appropriations for the improvement of all the other bays, inlets, and creeks, which may with equal propriety be called harbors, and of all the rivers, important or unimportant, in every part of the Union. To sanction the bill with such provisions would be to concede the *principle* that the Federal Government possesses the power to expend the public money in a general system of internal improvements, limited in its extent only by the ever-varying discretion of successive Congresses and successive Executives. It would be to efface and remove the limitations and restrictions of power which the Constitution has wisely provided to limit the authority and action of the Federal Government to a few well-defined and specified objects. Besides these objections, the practical evils which must flow from the exercise on the part of the Federal Government of the powers asserted in this bill impress my mind with a grave sense of my duty to avert them from the country as far as my constitutional action may enable me to do so.

It not only leads to a consolidation of power in the Federal Government at the expense of the rightful authority of the States, but its inevitable tendency is to embrace objects for the expenditure of the public money which are local in their character, benefiting but few at the expense of the common Treasury of the whole. It will engender sectional feelings and prejudices calculated to disturb the harmony of the Union. It will destroy the harmony which should prevail in our legislative councils.

It will produce combinations of local and sectional interests, strong enough when united to carry propositions for appropriations of public money which could not of themselves, and standing alone, succeed, and can not fail to lead to wasteful and extravagant expenditures.

It must produce a disreputable scramble for the public money, by the conflict which is inseparable from such a system between local and individual interests and the general interest of the whole. It is unjust to those States which have with their own means constructed their own internal improvements to make from the common Treasury appropriations for similar improvements in other States.

In its operation it will be oppressive and unjust toward those States whose representatives and people either deny or doubt the existence of the power or think its exercise inexpedient, and who, while they equally contribute to the Treasury, can not consistently with their opinions engage in a general competition for a share of the public money. Thus a large portion of the Union, in numbers and in geographical extent, contributing its equal proportion of taxes to the support of the Government, would under the operation of such a system be compelled to see the national treasure—the common stock of all—unequally disbursed, and often improvidently wasted for the advantage of small sections, instead of being applied to the great national purposes in which all have a common interest, and for which alone the power to collect the revenue was given. Should the system of internal improvements proposed prevail, all these evils will multiply and increase with the increase of the number of the States and the extension of the geographical limits of the settled portions of our country. With the increase of our numbers and the extension of our settlements the local objects demanding appropriations of the public money for their improvement will be proportionately increased. In each case the expenditure of the public money would confer benefits, direct or indirect, only on a section, while these sections would become daily less in comparison with the whole.

Should this bill become a law, the principle which it establishes will inevitably lead to large and annually increasing appropriations and drains upon the Treasury, for it is not to be doubted that numerous other localities not embraced in its provisions . . . will demand through their representatives in Congress, to be placed on an equal footing. . . . With such an increase of expenditure must necessarily follow either an increased public debt or increased burdens upon the people by taxation to supply the Treasury with the means of meeting the accumulated demands upon it.

What President . . . Ever Practiced
Such Small Intrigue?

Columbus *Ohio Statesman*

. . . We most warmly condemn the conduct of President Polk, in vetoing the river and harbor bill; and we have no hesitation in saying, that his course should be pointedly condemned by every western democrat. The message in which the President supports his views, is a shallow performance, vulgar in its language, ridiculous for its false logic, and paltry as the treatment of a thesis by some hair-splitting and wire-drawing schoolman of the middle ages, who thought himself a great man, because, like all small characters, he had mistaken cunning for wisdom. It is, however, quite worthy [of] the man whose imbecility has been so unhappily displayed in his action on the Oregon question— first uttering boasts of the loudest kind, and then sneaking off to cover when the enemy's bay was faintly heard in the distance. . . . So has he now vetoed a bill substantially recommended by himself, through the report of the Secretary of War. . . . Whoever heard of a high cabinet officer recommending to Congress . . . a course of action directly contrary to that of the President himself . . . whoever heard of anything of the kind, we ask, before these days of deception and palpable fraud? What President with a decent portion of self respect, ever practiced such small intrigue . . . ? As the great *words* about Oregon were followed by the smallest possible *actions,* and were intended only to gull honest men, so was the course of the President on the subject of improving harbors and rivers favorable, only with the design of gaining votes for the new tariff bill, the administration not having faith enough to believe that one righteous measure could stand without practicing a little falsehood on another. We most earnestly hope, that the day is not coming, when every true democrat will have, in bitterness of

Columbus *Ohio Statesman,* August 7, 1846.

heart, to ask pardon of God and man for having aided in elevating to
power, men who mistake treachery for good conduct, and paltry shifts
for great statesmanship.

. . . We have never seen any thing more exquisitely ridiculous,
than the President's assertion, that the appropriations for lakes' harbors
were not intended to facilitate foreign commerce! . . . How can we
export our productions to the Atlantic border, if our means of navigation are not improved? If we are to be left to nothing but the works of
nature, the Whig argument that we cannot compete with the grain
growers of Northern Europe and Southern Russia, becomes an admitted and indisputable fact. To improve lake harbors, is quite as necessary for the prosperity of foreign commerce, as it is to build light houses
on our eastern seaboard. The West is to be the great exporting quarter
of the Union, ultimately; but if it is to be cut off from all chances of
improvement, its people had better not "go ahead" quite so fast, as they
will otherwise be compelled to consume all they raise, despite the triumph of free trade principles and that would be bad *measure* indeed.
Perhaps, however, the President may think that the exports of the
country—always excepting cotton and tobacco—are miraculously fur-
nished to the merchants, pretty much as quails and manna were sent
to the Israelites, and that terrestrial measures are not needed to do that
so handsomely achieved by celestial means. In time, we do not despair
of even his learning his mistake, and of his being convinced of the
folly of the belief that the West has nothing to do with the foreign
trade of the country.

The plain truth is, that the veto of this measure of vital importance to our section of this republic, is but a carrying out of that harsh
and unjust policy towards the West, that the administration adopted
at the commencement of its existence, and which it has pursued until
now—consistent in this, if in nothing else—a policy which will coun-
tenance nothing likely to aid us, unless other parts are to reap more
from it than we do, and which confines appointments to office from
this region, with some exceptions, to places of third and fourth rate
character. We have been slow to believe in the existence of this hostile
feeling; but we should be more blind than the dead, were we not to see
it now, and more cowardly than we trust anything could make us, were
we not to denounce it with whatever power we may possess.

We are as much opposed to that vast and fantastic scheme of internal improvements advocated by the Whigs, as any man in the nation;

but we trust there is a medium between an extravagant scheme and absolutely doing nothing—a medium which real statesmanship can hit, and pursue, as much to their own honor as to the advantage of the nation. As to the ridiculous abstractions entertained by some portions of the South on this subject, we believe no one here regards them with more respect than the talk of the insane. We are a practical people, and we cannot understand why it is, that it is always unconstitutional to fit a western harbor for use, while millions upon millions can be expended upon northern and southern harbors, without the "sacred charter of our liberties" receiving the slightest infraction. It surpasses the comprehension of plain men, that it should be so deadly a wrong to spend a little money for the benefit of the West, while it is so very wise a thing to pour it out by oceans for the benefit of the East and the South.

. . . At the present time, the commerce of our great Western Lakes, or "Inland Seas," is estimated at one hundred millions of dollars per annum. . . . What a blessing it would be, could these grand *fresh water seas,* by some hocus-pocus, become so seasoned with salt as to overcome all "conscientious scruples," in high and low quarters.

source **26**

Ninth Resolution of the Chicago Rivers and Harbors Convention

That, in consequence of the peculiar dangers of the navigation of the Lakes, arising from the want of harbors for shelter, and of the Western Rivers from snags and other obstructions, there are no parts of the United States more emphatically demanding the prompt and con-

Robert Fergus, comp., *The Chicago River and Harbor Convention, 1847* (Chicago, 1882), p. 83.

tinued care of the Government to diminish those dangers, and to protect the life and property exposed to them; and that any one who can regard provisions for those purposes as sectional or local, and not national, must be wanting in information of the extent of the commerce carried on upon those lakes and rivers, and of the amount of teeming population occupied or interested in that navigation.

source **27**

This Bill Will Go Far to Demoralize
the People

James Buchanan

To the Senate of the United States:

I return with my objections to the Senate, in which it originated, the bill entitled "An act to secure homesteads to actual settlers on the public domain. . . . The facts raise the question whether Congress, under the Constitution, has the power to give away the public lands either to States or individuals. On this question I expressed a decided opinion in my message to the House of Representatives of the 24th February, 1859, returning the agricultural-college bill. This opinion remains unchanged. The argument then used applies as a constitutional objection with greater force to the present bill. *There* it had the plea of consideration, growing out of a specific beneficial purpose; *here* it is an absolute gratuity to the States, without the pretext of consideration. . . .

It would require clear and strong evidence to induce the belief that the framers of the Constitution, after having limited the powers of Congress to certain precise and specific objects, intended by employing the words "dispose of" to give that body unlimited power over the vast

James Buchanan's veto of the Homestead Bill, June 22, 1860, Richardson, *Messages and Papers,* VII, 3139-45.

public domain. It would be a strange anomaly indeed to have created two funds—the one by taxation, confined to the execution of the enumerated powers delegated to Congress, and the other from the public lands, applicable to all subjects, foreign and domestic, which Congress might designate; that this fund should be "disposed of," not to pay the debts of the United States, nor "to raise and support armies," nor "to provide and maintain a navy," nor to accomplish any one of the other great objects enumerated in the Constitution, but be diverted from them to pay the debts of the States, to educate their people, and to carry into effect any other measure of their domestic policy. This would be to confer upon Congress a vast and irresponsible authority utterly at war with the well-known jealousy of Federal power which prevailed at the formation of the Constitution. . . .

2. It will prove unequal and unjust in its operation among the actual settlers themselves.

The first settlers of a new country are a most meritorious class. They brave the dangers of savage warfare, suffer the privations of a frontier life, and with the hand of toil bring the wilderness into cultivation. . . .

This class have all paid for their lands the Government price, or $1.25 per acre. They have constructed roads, established schools, and laid the foundation of prosperous commonwealths. Is it just, is it equal, that after they have accomplished all this by their labor new settlers should come in among them and receive their farms at the price of 25 or 18 cents per acre . . . ?

4. This bill will prove unequal and unjust in its operation, because from its nature it is confined to one class of our people. It is a boon exclusively conferred upon the cultivators of the soil. Whilst it is cheerfully admitted that these are the most numerous and useful class of our fellow-citizens and eminently deserve all the advantages which our laws have already extended to them, yet there should be no new legislation which would operate to the injury or embarrassment of the large body of respectable artisans and laborers. . . .

5. This bill is unjust to the old States of the Union in many respects. . . . The offer of free farms would probably have a powerful effect in encouraging emigration, especially from States like Illinois, Tennessee, and Kentucky, to the west of the Mississippi, and could not fail to reduce the price of property within their limits. . . .

9. The effect of this bill on the public revenue must be apparent

to all. . . . The Secretary of the Interior estimated the revenue from the public lands for the next fiscal year at $4,000,000, on the presumption that the present land system would remain unchanged. Should this bill become a law, he does not believe that $1,000,000 will be derived from this source. . . .

The people of the United States have advanced with steady but rapid strides to their present condition of power and prosperity. They have been guided in their progress by the fixed principle of protecting the equal rights of all, whether they be rich or poor. No agrarian sentiment has ever prevailed among them. The honest poor man, by frugality and industry, can in any part of our country acquire a competence for himself and his family, and in doing this he feels that he eats the bread of independence. He desires no charity, either from the Government or from his neighbors. This bill, which proposes to give him land at an almost nominal price out of the property of the Government, will go far to demoralize the people and repress this noble spirit of independence. It may introduce among us those pernicious social theories which have proved so disastrous in other countries.

source **28**

The Policy That He Pursues . . .
Is Wrong

Mr. RICHARDSON. I am only desirous of saying, in relation to this matter, that I differ with the President of the United States in the views which he expresses on this question. . . . There can be no reason why, if Congress makes appropriations for improvements on the shore of the Atlantic and Pacific, it should not also make appropria-

Debate on Pierce's veto of the Rivers and Harbors Bill, August 5, 1854, *Congressional Globe*, 33rd Cong., 1st sess., pp. 2221-23.

tions for improvements in the interior. If you must have appropriations at all, let all share alike, all sections; if you are ready to quit all, I am with you.

The policy that he pursues of vetoing appropriations for interior improvements is wrong, if it is right to provide for those improvements any where. If we are to have appropriations for improvements upon the Atlantic and the Pacific, there is no reason why we should not have them in the interior. The Government becomes onerous to us, and unjust to us. It is wrong; I differ with him upon that point.

MR. BARKSDALE. I shall not enter into a discussion now, nor do I know that I shall do so at any other time, of the principles involved in the President's veto message. I wish, however, to notice a remark which fell from my friend from Illinois. We have heard of various combinations which have been recently formed in this country. Fusion between those who claimed to be Democrats and Whigs, Free-Soilers and Abolitionists. I have not been particularly astonished at these combinations and fusions and striking of hands. Nobody has been. But I must confess that I am somewhat astonished at the fusion we have witnessed here this morning, and I think the country will be astonished. Antipodes have met to-day. The gentleman from Ohio [Mr. Campbell] and the gentleman from Illinois [Mr. Richardson] have "struck hands" in the American Congress. I congratulate my friend from Illinois in the company he places himself in this morning. He has fought a gallant and a glorious battle during this session of Congress against the gentleman from Ohio and his friends. He gained the victory, but after the victory has been gained, he surrenders his arms, and we now find him in fond, affectionate, and loving embrace with the gentleman from Ohio. Now, however worthy my friend from Ohio, personally, may be, I should dislike very much to go to my Democratic constituents—my friend from Illinois can speak for himself, but we have cooperated together as Democrats here; I suppose a Democrat in Mississippi would be a Democrat in Illinois, and *vice versa*—I should dislike very much to go to my Democratic friends in Mississippi, and tell them that I had struck hands with the gentleman from Ohio. Now, I do not know how it may be with my friend from Illinois.

MR. RICHARDSON. It is all right.

MR. BARKSDALE. It may be all right with him, but it would not be all right with me. These are all the remarks I intended to make, and I will not detain the House any longer.

MR. RICHARDSON. I have but a single remark to make in reply to the gentleman from Mississippi [Mr. Barksdale]. He congratulates me that I find myself in company with strange bedfellows. I have laid down the position upon which I stand, and I stand there, I care not who stands with me, or who against me. I form my own opinion upon every subject, and I act upon that without regard to the opinion of anybody else. I repeat, here, to the House that I do not care what the President may think upon this, or that, or any other subject. The policy of the Government which allows appropriations to the sea-board, and claims them to be constitutional, and yet denies them to the interior, is wrong and unjust, and I condemn it. I do not care who goes with me. As for the positions which I take, I assume them for myself. The position which I take I assume for myself. I assume it here and elsewhere, and everywhere. I have voted on these principles. Nor are they the opinions of a day. When Congress determines to strike down appropriations for everything in the shape of public improvements, and to leave them entirely to the several States, when it discontinues its appropriations for New York, Philadelphia, Baltimore, New Orleans, and every other place, for light-houses, and buoys, and custom-houses, and coast surveys, I will then stand by the gentlemen who support this veto, and will go with them. But when gentlemen come and say, we are for these things, but we are against those things which are for the benefit of internal commerce, I denounce that policy as unjust and wrong. When you claim the right constitutionally to make appropriations for the seaboard, and deny the same to the interior, I do not care who stands with me or who stands against me, but I oppose that policy. I walk the track in opposition to it, and I care not whether I have to trudge it alone. The position I assume is just, it is right, and I will stand by it, I do not care who is against it or who is for it. When I go home and tell my constituents that I stand where General Jackson stood, it is no disgrace to me to say that the gentleman from Ohio [Mr. Campbell] follows in the wake of the lights laid down by him, and that he says it is right to follow him.

Now, I have one single thing further to say. I have said that if appropriations were to be made at all, I was in favor of appropriations for the improvement of the western rivers. And I may ask—and ask triumphantly—if the great Mississippi river is not a national stream—running through and touching, as it does, some ten States of this Union? What is the Atlantic more?

I Falter and I Hesitate

James Cavanaugh

Sir, the West has grown up in a wondrous manner. It has grown up, as it were, by magic. Take my own State for an example, if you please, for the last nine years. Why, sir, nine years ago the census of that State, then a Territory, was taken, and its population amounted to four thousand and some odd hundreds. Now, it is a sovereign State of this Union, numbering over two hundred thousand free, intelligent, and independent people—people who have gone there from the north, from the south, from the east, and from the west, carrying with them the institutions of the several States from which they emigrated; carrying with them the Bible, the rifle, the ax, the schoolhouse, and the church; carrying with them, also, the appliances of civilization. . . . From a struggling Territory, we have formed a great State, adding another jewel to the already splendid crown that gilds this western hemisphere! How has it been done? By your speculators, or by your actual settlers? Certainly not by the gentlemen who fight the bulls and bears on Wall street; not by the gentlemen who sell goods on India wharf in Boston; not by the individuals who deal in cotton on the levee in New Orleans; but by the brawny and strong arms of the laboring men who have gone there and rescued that Territory and its broad acres from a wild, but luxuriant growth, and brought them into cultivation; who have made those fertile prairies of ours bud and blossom like a rose, and our vast valleys vocal with the hum of the industry of an honest yeomanry. I am, sir, on this question of the public lands, perhaps intensely radical. . . . I speak the honest sentiments of my constituents, and I speak the honest sentiments of my

Representative James Cavanaugh, *Congressional Globe*, 35th Cong., 2d sess., 504-5.

heart, when I say that these public lands of ours belong to the people only, and to the men who will cultivate them. . . .

In reference to the vote on this bill today, with an overwhelming majority of this side of the House voting against my colleague and myself, voting against this bill, I say it frankly, I say it in sorrow, that it was to the Republican side of the House to whom we were compelled to look for support of this just and honest measure. Gentlemen from the South, gentlemen who have broad acres and wide plantations, aided here to-day, by their votes, more to make Republican States in the North than by any vote which has been cast within the last two years. These gentlemen ask us to come here and support the South; yet they, to a man almost, vote against the free, independent labor of the North and West.

I, sir, have inherited my Democracy; have been attached to the Democratic party from my boyhood; have believed in the great truths, as enunciated by the "fathers of the faith," and have cherished them religiously, knowing that, by their faithful application to every department of the Government, this nation has grown up from struggling colonies to prosperous, powerful, and sovereign States. But, sir, when I see southern gentlemen come up, as I did to-day, and refuse, by their votes, to aid my constituents, refuse to place the actual tiller of the soil, the honest, industrious laborer, beyond the grasp and avarice of the speculator, I tell you, sir, I falter and I hesitate. . . .

To the gentlemen on the Republican side of the House, who voted with my colleague and myself, I accord cheerfully the praise. I trust that as they have commenced, they will continue to pursue, the line of policy that will result in giving free homes to honest and industrious settlers. . . . I was not sent here to represent the Democratic party merely. My fealty to that party cannot be questioned. But I am also here with my colleague to represent the interests of two hundred thousand people of the Northwest; and when I fail to represent them honestly and faithfully, it is the simplest process for them to tell me that I have not discharged my trust. They can, in that event, make their voice known through the ballot; and their suffrages will fall silently as the snow-flake, but with the power and strength of majesty.

Economic Planks of the Republican Platform, 1860

12. That, while providing revenue for the support of the general government by duties upon imports, sound policy requires such an adjustment of these imports as to encourage the development of the industrial interests of the whole country; and we commend that policy of national exchanges, which secures to the workingmen liberal wages, to agriculture remunerative prices, to mechanics and manufacturers an adequate reward for their skill, labor, and enterprise, and to the nation commercial prosperity and independence.

13. That we protest against any sale or alienation to others of the public lands held by actual settlers, and against any view of the free-homestead policy which regards the settlers as paupers or suppliants for public bounty; and we demand the passage by Congress of the complete and satisfactory homestead measure which has already passed the House. . . .

15. That appropriations by Congress for river and harbor improvements of a national character, required for the accommodation and security of an existing commerce, are authorized by the Constitution, and justified by the obligation of Government to protect the lives and property of its citizens.

16. That a railroad to the Pacific Ocean is imperatively demanded by the interests of the whole country; that the federal government ought to render immediate and efficient aid in its construction; and that, as preliminary thereto, a daily overland mail should be promptly established.

Porter and Johnson, *op. cit.*, p. 33. Reprinted by permission.

To Hedge Against Divisions in the Republican Ranks; Abraham Lincoln to Schuyler Colfax

Springfield, Ills., July 6, 1859

My Dear Sir:

I regret much not seeing you while you were here among us. . . . Besides a strong desire to make your personal acquaintance, I was anxious to speak to you on politics. . . . My main object in such conversation would be to hedge against divisions in the Republican ranks generally, and particularly for the contest of 1860. The point of danger is the temptation in different localities to *"platform"* for something which will be popular just there, but which, nevertheless, will be a firebrand elsewhere, and especially in a National convention. As instances, the movement against foreigners in Massachusetts; in New-Hampshire, to make obedience to the Fugitive Slave law, punishable as a crime; in Ohio, to repeal the Fugitive Slave law; and squatter sovereignty in Kansas. In these things there is explosive matter enough to blow up half a dozen national conventions, if it gets into them; and what gets very rife outside of conventions is very likely to find it's way into them. What is desirable, if possible, is that in every local convocation of Republicans, a point should be made to avoid everything which will distract republicans elsewhere. Massachusetts republicans should have looked beyond their noses; and then they could not have failed to see that tilting against foreigners would ruin us in the whole North-West. New-Hampshire and Ohio should forbear tilting against the Fugitive Slave law in such way as [to] utterly overwhelm us in Illinois with the charge of enmity to the constitution itself. Kansas, in her confidence that she can be saved to freedom on "squatter sover-

Roy P. Basler, ed., *The Collected Works of Abraham Lincoln* (New Brunswick, N.J.: Rutgers University Press, 1953). Reprinted by permission.

eignty"—ought not to forget that to prevent the spread and nationalization of slavery is a national concern, and must be attended to by the nation. In a word, in every locality we should look beyond our noses; and at least say *nothing* on points where it is probable we shall disagree.

I write this for your eye only; hoping however that if you see danger as I think I do, you will do what you can to avert it. Could not suggestions be made to the leading men in the State and congressional conventions; and so avoid, to some extent at least, these apples of discord? Yours very truly

A. Lincoln

source 32

Some Considerable Trouble . . . Arose

Gustave Koerner

This party [the Know-Nothings] at least as regards the vote of the foreign-born population, had a very injurious influence in the coming election [in 1856]. It was supposed, and with some reason, that many of the Northern Know-Nothings on account of the slavery question, would join the Republican party without renouncing their hostility to all alien born, and might exercise thus a malignant influence on the Republican party. . . . Douglas made no speech in vindication of his course on the slavery question without improving the opportunity of recalling to mind the traditional liberal policy of the Democrats regarding aliens, and without denouncing most strongly the principles of the American party. Other Democratic speakers did the same, and they were justified in doing so. . . . It was quite natural, that under

Memoirs of Gustave Koerner 1809-1896 (Cedar Rapids, 1909), II, 20-21, 26-27, 74-76, 89-90.

the circumstances the voters of foreign birth, who had almost unanimously belonged to the Democratic party, should hesitate long before they joined a new party, among whom they recognized a great many people who had been always opposed to them. Yet the Germans were so much opposed to slavery that, with the exception of the Catholics amongst them, against whom the Know-Nothings had more particularly directed their assaults, it may be said that almost all marched to the polls under the Republican banner. Yet the Catholic element in many places was very strong, and the stand they took for the Pro-Slavery Democracy impaired the strength of the Republican party very greatly. . . .

[During the election] I was making a speech in the Mud Creek settlement. . . . All the settlers there . . . were . . . devoted Catholics and staunch Democrats. . . . The Democrats . . . had sent Francis J. Grund there . . . to keep the Germans straight. He eulogized . . . the Democratic party for their love of the alien-born, for their defense of the Catholics, and for their denunciation of the Know-Nothings. The Black Republicans . . . were made up, he said, principally of long-faced, white-livered, hypocritical Yankees, who sold wooden nutmegs and cheated the honest farmers with lightening rods and Yankee clocks. They would not allow a man to cook meals on the Sabbath, or kiss his wife, or take a walk for pleasure. Most of the Republicans were temperance people and hated the Germans because they would drink beer even on Sundays and would sing and dance on the Lord's day. Another part of the party were rank Abolitionists who would break up the Union, and another faction of them were Know-Nothings. Surely the people around him, who were good Catholics and were fond of a glass of lager, would not vote for such a party. Of course this was a very effective speech for that crowd. . . .

[In 1860] some considerable trouble . . . arose from the passage of an amendment to the Massachusetts Constitution, providing that naturalized citizens should not be allowed to vote or hold office until two years after the date of their naturalization. As the Republicans were supposed to have a majority in that State . . . the Democrats charged this unfriendly legislation against citizens of foreign birth upon the whole Republican party. Particularly the German element became much excited. The more radical German Republican press advised the German Republicans to punish the . . . party by voting at the next election for the Democrats. . . .

The great indignation felt by the Germans, and expressed in the entire German press with more or less vivacity . . . had . . . an excellent effect, [however]. Commencing with Ohio, in all the Northern states, the Republican State Convention most strongly expressed themselves against the spirit of the amendment. . . . [At the Republican convention in Chicago] our platform [contained a] . . . resolution opposing any change in the naturalization laws, and disapproving of any act of State legislatures to impair the rights of naturalized citizens. . . . Among the delegates from Massachusetts . . . was John A. Andrews. . . . At first he paid no particular attention to the debate on the resolution; but when Massachusetts was mentioned as being the State whose action was disapproved, he turned around to Boutwell . . . on his left, and exclaimed: "That will never do! This is aimed at our State." And with that he rose, and called out: "Mr. President!" He being a man of great influence, it is hard to tell what might have become of the resolution. . . . But Boutwell . . . who had become convinced that this very section was all important to keep the German-Republicans in line, at once laid hands on Andrews's shoulders and sought to push him down, while I, sitting right behind him, took hold of his coat tails and held him down; and while he was looking around with the greatest astonishment . . . the vote was taken on the resolution and the next one was read.

We Do Not Seek to Force,
or Even to Intrude,
Our Systems on You

William H. Seward

Suppose we had the power to change your social system: what warrant have you for supposing that we should carry negro equality among you . . . ? I am no assailant of States. . . . we do not seek to force, or even to intrude, our system on you. We are excluded justly, wisely, and contentedly, from all political power and responsibility in your capital States. You are sovereign on the subject of slavery within your own borders, as we are on the same subject within our borders. It is well and wisely so arranged. Use your authority to maintain what system you please. We are not distrustful of the result. We have wisely, as we think, exercised ours to protect and perfect the manhood of the members of the State. The whole sovereignty upon domestic concerns within the Union is divided between us by unmistakable boundaries. You have your fifteen distinct parts; we eighteen parts, equally distinct. Each must be maintained in order that the whole may be preserved. If ours shall be assailed, within or without, by any enemy, or for any cause, and we shall have need, we shall expect you to defend it. If yours shall be so assailed, in the emergency, no matter what the cause or the pretext, or who the foe, we shall defend your sovereignty as the equivalent of our own. We cannot, indeed, accept your system of capital or its ethics. That would be to surrender and subvert our own, which we esteem to be better. Besides, if we could, what need for any division into States at all? You are equally at liberty to reject our system and its ethics, and to maintain the superiority of your own by all the forces of persuasion and argument. We must, indeed, mutually

William H. Seward, February 29, 1860, *Congressional Globe,* 36th Cong., 1st sess., 912-14.

discuss both systems. All the world discusses all systems. Especially must we discuss them since we have to decide as a nation which of the two we ought to ingraft on the new and future States growing up in the great public domain. Discussion then being unavoidable, what could be more wise than to conduct it with mutual toleration and in a fraternal spirit . . . ?

I can pronounce as accurately concerning the northern or Republican representatives here as anyone. I know their public haunts and their private ways. We are not a hostile Republic, or representative of one. We confer together, but only as the organs of every party do, and must do in a political system which obliges us to act sometimes as partisans, while it requires us always to be patriots and statesmen. Differences of opinion, even on the subject of slavery, with us are political, not social or personal differences. There is not one disunionist or disloyalist among us all. We are altogether unconscious of any process of dissolution going on among us or around us. We have never been more patient, and never loved the representatives of other sections more, than now. We bear the same testimony for the people around us here, who, though in the very center where the bolt of disunion must fall first and be most fearful in its effects, seem never less disturbed than now. We bear the same testimony for all the districts and States we represent. The people of the North are not enemies but friends and brethren of the South, faithful and true as in the days when death has dealt his arrows promiscuously among them on common battle-fields of freedom. . . .

The method we have adopted, of appealing to the reason and judgment of the people, to be pronounced by suffrage, is the only one by which free government can be maintained anywhere, and the only one as yet devised which is in harmony with the spirit of the Christian religion. While generous and charitable natures will probably concede that John Brown and his associates acted on earnest though fatally erroneous convictions, yet all good citizens will nevertheless agree, that this attempt to execute an unlawful purpose in Virginia by invasion, involving servile war, was an act of sedition and treason, and criminal in just the extent that it affected the public peace and was destructive of human happiness and human life. It is a painful reflection that, after so long an experience of the beneficent working of our system as we have enjoyed, we have had these new illustrations in Kansas and Virginia of the existence among us of a class of men so misguided and so desperate as to seek to enforce their peculiar principles by the sword. . . .

Who believes that a Republican administration and Congress could practice tyranny under a Constitution which interposes as many checks as ours? Yet that tyranny must not only be practiced, but must be intolerable, and there must be no remaining hope for constitutional relief, before forcible resistance can find ground to stand on anywhere.

The people of the United States, acting in conformity with the Constitution, are the supreme tribunal to try and determine all political issues. They are as competent to decide the issues of today as they have been heretofore to decide the issues of other days. They can reconsider hereafter and reverse, if need be, the judgment they shall pronounce to-day, as they have more than once reconsidered and reversed their judgments in former times. It needs no revolution to correct any error, or prevent any danger, under any circumstances.

Nor is any new or special cause for revolution likely to occur under a Republican administration. We are engaged in no new transaction, not even in a new dispute.

source **34**

Old Issues Are Dead and Gone

Henry Hilliard

. . . I assure you, gentlemen, that I am no less an advocate of conservative principles and counsels which I esteem prudent to-day, than when you and I stood together under the standard of that grand . . . patriotic party, stern in its defense of the Constitution, and loyal to the whole country—the WHIG party. So long as it maintained its

Henry Hilliard to the Editor, Washington *National Intelligencer*, June 2, 1857.

organization I shared its fortunes, prosperous or adverse, unflinchingly confident in its principles, proud of its triumphs, undismayed by its defeats. But the great contest through which the country has just passed brought about a change in party alliances, and men hitherto sundered and antagonistical found themselves brought into new relations to each other. The Black Republican party was very formidable; its batallions hung in threatening masses along the whole North and Northwest. They were confronted by the Democratic party under the lead of Mr. Buchanan, and by a considerable body of conservative men who gave their support to Mr. Fillmore. My old Whig partialities, my personal regard for Mr. Fillmore, and my confidence in his wisdom and patriotism—both of which I had seen before—led me into the ranks of his supporters; but I always insisted that the Government might be entrusted safely either to him or to Mr. Buchanan. The Democratic party, with the aid of conservative men outside of its ranks, succeeded in electing their candidate; and in his Inaugural address, Mr. Buchanan announced the policy of the incoming Administration in terms which met my approbation. I do not regard it as an unmeaning speech, but coming from a statesman of great weight of character, ripe in age and experience. . . . Urged to become a candidate for Congress, I declined to be such if I must return there to oppose an Administration which I hoped and believed would deserve a cordial, generous and unbroken support from the Southern people.

. . . I claim to be national; and I therefore recommend to my former constituents a firm and unstinted support of an Administration which, in my judgment, is eminently patriotic and which will do whatever can be done by wise and just measures to strengthen and uphold the Government. Why should not the South unite in support of Mr. Buchanan's Administration? Why should you or I, gentlemen, oppose it? What is there in the programme already given to the country to encourage or justify opposition to it?

I have said, what I do not hesitate to say again, that the Free Soil party is not scattered; that I believe it will rally for the next Presidential election with more formidable strength and more dangerous purposes than it has yet exhibited; and I have said, what I once more say with, if possible, added emphasis, that in my judgment the Administration, standing as a bulwark for the defence of our rights ought to be sustained by the *"undivided South."*

Far, very far, from desiring to encourage geographic distinctions

. . . I cannot overlook the fact that the South, as the weaker section, cannot afford to divide its strength. It ought to present an unbroken front. . . . *An undivided South as the base of a great Constitutional party, embracing the conservative men of all sections, is what I desire to see.* . . . Is it not wise to rescue the Government from the hands of men who base their claims to power upon a . . . purpose to turn the whole energies of a common political system against a section, its property, and its institutions?

What have we got to gain by opposing Mr. Buchanan's Administration, or by weakening the Democratic party? Old issues are dead and gone; the living questions are before us, and in regard to these I am at a loss to see how the conservative men of any part of the country can make war upon the Administration. . . . We must learn to conquer our prejudices; we must yield our support to just measures wherever we find them, and we must give our confidence to men who stood with us in the late struggle against the formidable hosts which disputed the field so severely. . . .

The brilliant victory achieved by the Democratic party, with the cooperation of the conservative men of other parties, has brought us into relations with each other which leave no room for former jealousies and ancient prejudices. The era of good feelings has, I trust, really come, and henceforth we should support an Administration borne into power by the late triumph of the friends of the Constitution— appealing as it does so nobly to the confidence of the country by the wisdom of its projected measures, whether we consider their domestic or foreign bearing. . . .

I Want No Fellowship with Your Organization

Mr. Benjamin [D-Louisiana]. Up to the years 1857 and 1858, no man in this nation had a higher or more exalted opinion of the character, the services, and the political integrity of the Senator from Illinois than I had. . . .

It has been with reluctance and sorrow that I have been obliged to pluck down my idol from his place on high, and to refuse to him any more support or confidence as a member of the party. I have done so, I trust, upon no light or unworthy ground. . . . We have separated from him, not because he held principles in 1856 different from ours. We have separated from him, not because we are intolerant of opposition from anybody, for the Senator from Ohio [Mr. Pugh] is an honored member of our organization. We separated from him because he has denied the bargain that he made when he went home, because, after telling us here in the Senate that he was willing that this whole matter should be decided by the Supreme Court, in the face of his people he told them that he had got us by the bill; and that, whether the decision was for us or against us, the practical effect was to be against us; and because he tells us now again that he is ready to make use of Black Republican arguments, which he answers at home, and to put them forth against the Democratic party in the speeches that he uses here in the Senate. . . .

Senator Pugh [D-Ohio]. You have made it a question of personal honor, and there you cannot stand. If we cannot remain in the organization of the Democratic party, exercising our judgment and will, according to the rules of the party; if when we are in the minority with

Comments in the Senate on the Split in the Democratic Party, May 22, 1860, *Congressional Globe,* 36th Cong., 1st sess., 2240-41, 2247-48.

our candidates rejected, with our declarations of principles ignored, we are called on to stand firm, and to fight the Opposition in every shape year after year—to fight even against hope—then, sir, when, by the established rules of the party, we come to have a majority, to be able to make our declarations of principles, and to nominate our candidates, you claim the right to tear the convention in pieces, I tell you to tear it; claim the right to set up another organization—set it up. I want no fellowship with your organization. I am not a candidate for admission into it. Now that you have left us, if you intend to stand upon that sort of usage, very well. I say this: if you demand that you shall have your way; that, whether a majority or minority, you shall govern; that no Democrat from any northern State shall presume to have any opinion, or to vote for any candidates, until he has got the leave of Louisiana, Alabama, and Mississippi, and the rest of those States—if those are the terms of union, I want it made known now. I believe my people do understand them now. . . .

Mr. WIGFALL [D-Texas]. It has never been to us a matter of any consequence who should administer the Government but the Senator from Ohio seems to predicate his fealty to the party upon that question. The question with us has been, how shall the Government be administered? and when that ceases to be the question, then I cease to feel any interest in the question, by whom is the Government to be administered? The Democratic party has been supposed to be one of principle. It has been supposed to be a party that was in favor of administering this Government in a particular manner, because they believed that, according to the Constitution, this Government was vested only with certain powers, and could, therefore, only exercise certain powers. With these views, the Democratic party through the different States of this Union—of which States this Government is a mere department or agent —met . . . supposing that we belonged to a party, which party was acting upon a certain set of principles; and if they are not acting upon those, then there is no party. . . .

Mr. Buchanan, in his inaugural address, announced precisely the doctrines which we now stand by. In his letter accepting the nomination he announced, as we understood it, and as we said, precisely the doctrines we now insist upon. I am not coming to the last message; but I say that in his letter of acceptance we understood him to announce the doctrines that we now advocate and insist upon; and that in his inaugural address he announced them so that the wayfaring man, though a fool, could not misunderstand. . . .

MR. PUGH. I understood, and I had some occasion to pay attention to it at that time—why I shall not say—that Mr. Buchanan expressed it as his opinion that they could only act upon the subject in forming a State constitution; but he acknowledged that it was an open question, and to be decided by the Supreme Court of the United States.

MR. WIGFALL. And I say the Supreme Court has decided.

MR. PUGH. That is the whole point of the controversy. The Senator then substitutes a question of fact for a question of principle. He has undertaken to divide the Democratic party because we are not all able to understand a particular decision alike, well knowing that a dozen lawyers sitting down to construe a decision might very well come to different conclusions.

Suggested Readings

The literature on the politics of the two decades before the Civil War is massive. Particularly useful general surveys of the period include Allen Nevins, *Ordeal of the Union* (New York: Charles Scribner's Sons, 1947-1950), 4 vols.; and Avery O. Craven, *The Coming of the Civil War,* 2nd Ed. (Chicago: University of Chicago Press, 1957). Neither stresses all that I have discussed here but both contain a great deal of relevant information on the political events of the period. Craven is particularly good in his chapters on the reactions of the West to the failure of the Democratic party to accept an extensive internal improvements program. Robert Rayback, *Millard Fillmore: The Biography of a President* (Buffalo: The Buffalo Historical Society, 1959) is a good study of a prominent Whig leader in the forties who became the Know-Nothing candidate for President in 1856.

The nature of political behavior and the role and importance of political parties in this period is well covered in Richard P. McCormick, *The Second American Party System* (Chapel Hill, N.C.: The University of North Carolina Press, 1966); and Lee Benson, *The Concept of Jacksonian Democracy: New York as a Test Case* (Princeton: Princeton University Press, 1961). Joel H. Silbey, *The Shrine of Party: Congressional Voting Behavior, 1841-1852* (Pittsburgh: University of Pittsburgh Press, 1967) examines the impact of political parties on a major institution of governmental activity. A challenging examination of American political behavior and the importance of parties in current American politics is Angus Campbell, *et al., The American Voter* (New York: John Wiley & Sons, Inc., 1960).

One can profitably begin the study of cultural conflict in American politics with Seymour Martin Lipset, "Religion and Politics in the American Past and Present," in Robert Lee and Martin Marty, *Religion and Social Conflict* (New York: Oxford University Press, 1964). Various aspects of the crisis of immigration, reform, and politics is touched on in different ways in Alice Felt Tyler, *Freedom's Ferment* (New York: Harper and Row, Publishers, 1942); Clifford Griffin, *Their Brother's Keepers* (New Brunswick, N.J.: Rutgers University Press, 1960); Timothy Smith, *Revivalism and Social Reform in Mid-Nineteenth Century America* (New York: Abingdon Press, 1958); Joseph Gusfield, *Symbolic Crusade* (Urbana: University of Illinois Press, 1963); Ray Billington, *The Protestant Crusade* (New York: The Macmillan Co., 1938); Whitney Cross, *The Burned-Over District* (Ithaca, N.Y.: Cornell University Press, 1957); Oscar Handlin, *Boston's Immigrants*, Rev. Ed. (Cambridge: Harvard University Press, 1959); John A. Krout, *The Origins of Prohibition* (New York: Alfred A. Knopf, Inc., 1925); and Frank Byrne, *Prophet of Prohibition: Neal Dow and His Crusade* (Madison, Wisc.: University of Wisconsin Press, 1961). Useful articles include David Davis, "Some Themes of Counter-Subversion," *Mississippi Valley Historical Review,* XLVII (September, 1960), 205-24; George Daniels, "Immigrant Vote in the 1860 Election: The Case of Iowa," *Mid-America,* XLIV (July, 1962), 146-62; and the old but quite perceptive, Joseph Schafer, "The Yankee and Teuton in Wisconsin," *Wisconsin Magazine of History,* VII (December, 1923), 148-71. Neal Dow, *The Reminiscences of Neal Dow* (Portland, Me.: Evening Express Publishing Co., 1898), should be consulted for its evocation of much of the flavor of the temperance movement.

Historians have dealt extensively with the slavery-extension controversy's effect on politics. A general survey of the subject is Louis Filler, *The Crusade Against Slavery* (New York: Harper and Row, Publishers, 1957). See also, Martin Duberman, ed., *The Anti-Slavery Vanguard* (Princeton, N.J.: Princeton University Press, 1965). Biographies of many of the men at the center of the controversy provide much useful material. See, particularly, Frank Otto Gatell, *John Gorham Palfrey and the New England Conscience* (Cambridge: Harvard University Press, 1963); Richard H. Sewell, *John P. Hale and the Politics of Abolition* (Cambridge: Harvard University Press, 1965); David Donald, *Charles Sumner and the Coming of the Civil War* (New York: Alfred A. Knopf, Inc., 1960); and Martin Duberman, *Charles Francis Adams, 1807-1886* (Boston: Houghton Mifflin Co., 1961).

The available materials concerning the role of economic controversy in American politics in this period is not as extensive as in the other two areas mentioned here. For the general background see Carter Goodrich, *Government Promotion of American Canals and Railroads, 1800-1890* (New York: Columbia University Press, 1960), and Robert Lively, "The American System: A Review Article," *Business History Review,* XXIX (March, 1955), 81-96. Some of the political aspects of the situation are dealt with in Don Fehrenbacher, *Chicago Giant: A Biography of 'Long John' Went-*

worth (Madison: American History Research Center, 1957); Charles G. Sellers, Jr., *James K. Polk, Continentalist, 1843-1846* (Princeton, N.J.: Princeton University Press, 1966); Charles Wiltse, *John C. Calhoun, Sectionalist, 1840-1850* (Indianapolis: The Bobbs-Merrill Co., 1951); and in Avery Craven's volume noted above. Two articles of merit are Mentor L. Williams, "The Background of the Chicago River and Harbor Convention, 1847," *Mid-America*, XXX (October, 1948), 219-32; and, by the same author, "The Chicago River and Harbor Convention, 1847," *Mississippi Valley Historical Review*, XXXIV (March, 1949), 607-26.

The rise of the Republicans and the decline of the Democrats is dealt with in many volumes. See, particularly, James G. Randall, *Lincoln The President, Springfield to Gettysburg* (New York: Dodd, Mead and Company, 1945), 2 volumes; Roy F. Nichols, *The Disruption of the American Democracy* (New York; The Macmillan Co., 1948); Gerald Capers, *Stephen A. Douglas, Defender of the Union* (Boston: Little, Brown and Co., 1959). All of these stress the slavery issue as the main circumstance in the party change, but they are also concerned with some of the other problems that I have dealt with here.